CRAP DAYS OUT

CRAP DAYS OUT

GARETH RUBIN

WITH CONTRIBUTIONS BY
JON PARKER

JOHN BLAKE

Published by John Blake Publishing Ltd,
3 Bramber Court, 2 Bramber Road,
London W14 9PB, England

www.johnblakepublishing.co.uk

www.facebook.com/Johnblakepub facebook
twitter.com/johnblakepub **twitter**

First published in hardback in 2011

ISBN: 978 1 84358 405 6

British Library Cataloguing-in-Publication Data:

A catalogue record for this book is available from the British Library.

Design by www.envydesign.co.uk

Printed and bound by CPI Group (UK) Ltd, Croydon, CR0 4YY

1 3 5 7 9 10 8 6 4 2

Papers used by John Blake Publishing are natural,
recyclable products made from wood grown in sustainable forests.
The manufacturing processes conform to the environmental
regulations of the country of origin.

Every attempt has been made to contact the relevant
copyright-holders, but some were unobtainable. We would be
grateful if the appropriate people could contact us.

CONTENTS

CONTENTS

INTRODUCTION

There's no getting around the fact: we are a nation who love a rubbish day out.

Other countries might be content to spend their holidays relaxing in the sun with friends and family, but we in Great Britain know that the only way to spend one of our rare bank holidays is to get up early and spend half the day driving to a tourist attraction that is worse than even our most cautious expectations.

So from childhood we are raised to expect the dire. With every trip to Stonehenge, Madame Tussauds or the York Quilt Museum our parents were saying: 'Son, this is what your weekends are going to be like from now on – just a bit crap. So don't get your hopes up.'

But we don't learn – because we don't want to. In adult life we dutifully keep up the tradition of inflicting painful days out on ourselves. From getting naked on our freezing beaches to visiting museums entirely about pencils, we seek them out like truffles in the soil. Maybe it's just part of our culture, maybe we do it so we look forward to going back to work on Monday – but for whatever reason, rubbish days out are part of who we are.

So the sites and attractions in this book are the ones you will be going to whether you like it or not. And you might as well go into it with your eyes open – after all, forewarned is forearmed. Join us.

THE SOUTH WEST

STONEHENGE
WILTSHIRE

A very nice piece of henge-work this – all those huge pieces of rock which were dragged halfway across the country with nothing more than a few sticks and brutal repercussions for anyone who questioned what *on earth* it was all for.

It's no surprise that people from all over the world flock to see this memoir of just how much time Neolithic man had on his hands for DIY and standing rocks on their ends. For anyone who has been there, it is also no surprise to know that the most common visitor's reaction is: 'Is that it then? Seriously? Bollocks, we should have gone to Bath after all. Oh, stop nagging.'

The thing is, there is a gap – a yawning chasm, really – between an amazing effort and amazing results. You can spend your lifetime building, dismantling and then rebuilding a twice-life-size model of Chairman Mao out of Wrigley's Juicy Fruit but at the end of the day, all you are left with is a massive piece of chewing gum. In the case of Stonehenge, you are left with 20-odd long rocks, some standing on top of the others, others just lazing about doing nothing. The latter group are known as 'teenage' stones.

The whole thing took more than 1,500 years to construct, although the builders had said it would be three weeks at the outside. First they dithered for 200 years because it looked like rain, and then the materials turned up 400 years late because they had to come from the other depot, and by that time they had to leave for another project they had booked on the early Triassic period land mass of Pangea. Well, we've all had little building projects that overran.

Yes, the Druids had a right bunch of cowboys in to do the work by the looks of things. They should have had a word with

Neolithic Crypto-Religious Construction Project Trading Standards. ('Hello, Trading Standards, can I help you? It's what? Oh not another bloody henge, we've had three complaints about henges this Bronze Age already. I'll be honest with you, mate, I've got henges coming out of me ears.')

No one really knows what the stone circle was for, although fragments of human bone, woven material and evidence of ropes suggest it could have been either a place for ceremonial cremation or an early all-in wrestling ring. One thing is for certain: whoever built it was very keen on ditches.

For many it truly is a spiritual experience to walk around the rope around the stone circle. They hear the stones speaking to them. Usually they say: 'You have wasted your morning.'

Adding to the experience, the site's owner, English Heritage, makes everyone change into druidic robes upon arrival and insists you take part in the Ceremony of the Four Winds in order to get into the spirit of things.

Ha ha! Only joking – that would be mental.

But it's definitely the place to be if you are into big static rocks, some vertical, others more horizontal.

Or you could just look at it all in a book.

In fact, luckily, you don't need to tramp through the muddy field that holds the rocks in order to be close enough to throw stuff at them like most bored visiting children. You can do that from the comfort of your car since the busy A303 and the furiously busy A344 intersect within spitting distance of the stones, providing a lively sonic backdrop to the scene. This ensures that you will never get bored by any of that dull silence which could distract you from getting in touch with your inner pagan. Or alien or Thetan or whatever other intergalactic species you believe had nothing better to do with their tractor beams than stand a bunch of rocks upright in a field near Salisbury.

Above all, Stonehenge is a place steeped in mystery, raising deep questions, such as: 'Is *Inspector Morse* on TV tonight?' 'Shall we leave?' and 'What's the quickest route to Bristol?'

THE DINOSAUR MUSEUM
DORCHESTER
DORSET

With an impressive average of one star out of five on the popular travel website Tripadvisor, Dorchester's Dinosaur Museum has its work cut out in living up to the hype.

One of the main talking points is the notable lack of dinosaurs in the museum, whether alive or dead. Few visitors had expectations of the former, but a smattering of the latter would not have gone amiss. Instead the museum apparently features a number of plastic toys similar to those widely available at your local market, and a costume which was once in an episode of *Doctor Who*. That is one of the old series of *Doctor Who* before it became ironic. The whole place seemingly evokes a strong sense of being in someone's spare room. Perhaps it is also a mistake to show *Jurassic Park* on permanent loop, since it only serves to remind visitors of what can be done with a substantial budget and a certain degree of effort.

Here is just a selection of the comments on Tripadvisor:

'The only thing correct on any of the leaflets is the address. I can imagine that the only award this place ever got was for worst attraction. Papier mâché old tatty models, bits of junk in boxes to feel, no real dinosaurs, and the sound effect of a dinosaur was an old bike horn. All in a room no bigger than half a tennis court. No staff except one miserable and rude woman doing both tickets and shop. Took my dino mad son who asked if we could go somewhere else after five minutes.' AMW

'I'd rather go the dentist than back to this place. Styles itself as Britain's Premier Dinosaur Museum. It's not even the premier dinosaur museum in its street.' Harbottle

'I paid £17 for three of us to go into someone's house and look at plastic toys nailed to the wall, and put our hands in a box with feathers in it. I could have done that at home.' CC Speakman

'We were out in minutes.' Helen

'Can't think what they are spending the money on. Certainly not on air-conditioning. The upstairs rooms were like a sauna, despite it being a cold, wet day. One of the most memorably bad exhibits was a plastic box on which was written the question "T. Rex is viewed as the king of the dinosaurs. Which animal is today's equivalent?" Inside was a plastic lion, with a leg missing, nailed to the floor of the box.' WorthingTruthSeeker

'When we asked what their refund policy was having been round it twice in about eight minutes the woman at the counter looked like she'd seen the ghost of a severely hacked off T-Rex.' Scatman

'"Interactive" means you can poke some more holes in the paper models. Avoid it. If you don't believe me, stand outside and look at the faces of people coming out before you make a decision.' Idratherbesleeping

'You would be better served burning a £20 note which would be wildly more entertaining and much better value for money.' Bidsky

COOPERS HILL CHEESE ROLLING
GLOUCESTERSHIRE

It's hard to say just why Gloucestershire is the world centre for rolling big cheeses down hills, but the world centre for rolling big cheeses it is. It may sound like a surreal 1960s TV series – young men screaming in terror as they are chased by giant Double Gloucesters – but it has been going on for an oddly long time. And the injuries have stacked up.

Oddly, the master of ceremonies at the rolling wears a top hat and white coat which make him look like a cross between a cheese salesman and an undertaker. He could be the one who sold you that cheese in Tesco today and you have to wonder what he secretly did to the cheese while it was out of your sight before he handed it over to you with a big grin.

In 1998 the event was cancelled because the year before there had been 33 recorded injuries. But don't worry, it was quickly reinstated. As one furious local resident said: 'This is the nanny state gone mad. If you can't hurl yourself down a steep hill after a few drinks chasing cheeses, what's the point in being British?' It's hard to known if he was being ironic.

On the bright side, the cheese rolling can be a useful aid for schools wanting to illustrate how natural selection works.

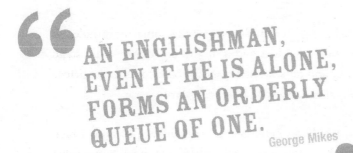

AN ENGLISHMAN, EVEN IF HE IS ALONE, FORMS AN ORDERLY QUEUE OF ONE. George Mikes

GLASTONBURY TOR
SOMERSET

Glastonbury Tor in Somerset is the centre of a magical realm where ley lines meet and the powers of the ancient earth goddess … oh hang on, that's all bollocks.

While many destinations featured in this book rest their appeal on some pretty spurious grounds, Glastonbury Tor pulls the crowds based on the fact that it is the last resting place of King Arthur – and it's magic. Actually magic.

The Tor is a hill outside Glastonbury village, at the top of which is St Michael's tower, a small building without a roof that, while quite nice, is still just a small building without a roof. People in shanty towns throughout the world have these and few find the time to boast about them.

> " I GET SO IMMODERATELY SICK OF BATH.
>
> Jane Austen, *Northanger Abbey* "

GLASTONBURY SYMPOSIUM
SOMERSET

An annual event dedicated to deciding whether crop circles are
the product of super-intelligent aliens who have nothing better
to do than nip over here and mark shapes in wheat... or of
bored students who think it will be a bit of a laugh. Every year
attendees come from all over the world to discuss this. We can
tell you now, the aliens theory isn't looking too strong.

THE GLASTONBURY FESTIVAL
SOMERSET

The hippy movement born in 1960s California was never going to translate wholly effectively to Britain, where the carefree spirit of sunny San Francisco was dampened – both metaphorically and literally – by this country's ever-present rain.

And nowhere is this clearer than at Britain's answer to Woodstock: the Glastonbury Festival, the biggest greenfield music festival in the world and where when it rains, it pours.

Like a message direct from God about the sins of free love and wearing tie-died T-shirts, Glastonbury rain is unceasing, remorseless, build-yourself-an-ark-and-start-gathering-animals type rain. And where rain leads, mud follows. In 1997, the muddiest festival year to date, torrential rain both during and preceding the festival turned the event into a scene resembling the Somme, only without the Red Cross packages or letters of encouragement from home. And with much worse food.

The other chief difference between Glastonbury and The Somme was that at least in the First World War you knew who the enemy was. At Glastonbury, the enemy is in your midst. He is from Liverpool, he is wearing a tracksuit, and he is stealing things from your tent while you are off cheering Muse.

By 2002, the festival had an average attendance of 250,000 despite ticket sales of 100,000; even a hippy can do that maths. So the site owner, festival organiser and God lookalike Michael Eavis called in Mean Fiddler to sort things out.

As well as the deployment of a team of jobbing bouncers, the company's surprisingly obvious solution to the security problem was to put up a massive fence. This means that even though it might not have the First World War mud of previous years, it does at least offer the chance to meet an untimely death caught in a web of barbed wire.

As well as clearing off the scallies, however, the security crackdown has also cleared off the aged hippies, bearded magic mushroom sellers and other eccentrics that made the festival what it was; as well as all the young people. The crowd at Glastonbury these days is full of thirtysomethings bringing luxury camper vans and gazebos, folding chairs and yurts. People bring their kids, drink rose wine from a box and there is a long queue at the stall charging £8 for a 'gourmet' pie. It makes you nostalgic for the days when you could open a warm Stella, buy a fiver's worth of hash from a crusty and try to dance to some Dutch techno.

Now ticket-holders are required to show their passport to enter. This means that entering the festival is much like entering the country – you pay a lot of money for a ticket, present your passport and enter, only to find that it's a small rainy place where everyone has a tiny home and hardly anyone is working.

Sadly there will be no festival in 2012, with Michael Eavis blaming it on there not being enough police available for everyone to have a really good time.

THE ENGLISH DON'T LIKE MUSIC, THEY JUST LIKE THE NOISE IT MAKES.

Sir Thomas Beecham

CERNE ABBAS GIANT
DORSET

UFFINGTON WHITE HORSE
OXFORDSHIRE

It's an odd idea: come to visit something you can't actually see unless you are 130ft tall. Is anyone that tall? We're not; not even combined. So unless you are on the world's highest and most precarious pair of stilts, clinging on for dear life and screaming that you have changed your mind about all this, you're just not going to see either of these two chalk outline figures very slightly carved out of the grass.

No one is sure if the white horse is even a horse. It might be a dog or a sparrow or something. Intriguingly, the ancient ... well, whoever it was who marked out the unidentified creature, left one leg floating away from the rest of his body, rather like Penfold's eyebrows in *Danger Mouse*.

And just what it is doing there on the side of a hill is also a bit sketchy. Some historians say it was carved in celebration of King Alfred's victory over the Danes in AD 871:

'Nice one, Alfred. So, how do you fancy celebrating?'

'I want a sodding massive white horse carved into a hill.'

'Really?'

'Yes.'

Then there's that giant. No one would dispute that children love giants – they go ape-shit for them. They are, after all, GIANTS. But aside from the anger, the smashing things etc., the point about giants is that they're supposed to be more visible than ordinary people, not less. So kids won't find this giant exciting unless they want their heads examined – which, of course, they might do after they fall off those massive stilts of yours. Honestly, I don't know why you brought them.

No one knows the reason for the giant's existence, either,

although it might have been carved to annoy Oliver Cromwell who was known to have an aversion to giants with clubs.

But the most interesting thing about the Cerne Abbas Giant is the size of his weapon. A euphemism? You betcha. If you like your giants with huge erect penises, this is certainly the giant for you. On the other hand, in these paranoid times, visiting the Cerne Abbas Giant with children – especially those to whom you are not directly related – is fraught with the distinct possibility that the wrong word could land you on the sex offenders register.

WINDMILL HILL CITY FARM
BRISTOL

As the name suggests, Windmill Hill City Farm is a farm in a city. In other words, it's a farm to be visited by city people who can't be bothered to go to the countryside to see a proper one. Beyond that, its slogan is 'A place where people grow', demonstrating that they have clearly misunderstood the purpose of a farm.

Continuing the questionable phrasing of its own raison d'être, its mission statement includes: 'To meet the needs of local people regardless of age, race, sex, disability, and social or economic circumstances', which surprises anyone who had presumed they would operate a strictly racist admittance policy, sexually harass women upon entry, and make 'spazmo' gestures at any working-class children in wheelchairs.

Like many a substitute, however, city farms bear little resemblance to the real thing. First, city farms raise a small number of animals that have been given cuddly names and are lovingly looked after by staff. Real farms, by contrast, produce a multitude of faceless animals to be slaughtered in their thousands by industrial killing machines while humans stand about reading the paper and occasionally pressing the button marked 'faster'.

To someone who works at a city farm, each animal has personality, each cow has an old-fashioned girl's name and each chicken, duck or goose is a feathered friend. To a real farmer, each animal has a cost and a sale price, and every chicken is a unit comprising 2.7 kievs and half a can of Whiskas.

Another important difference between city farms and real ones is that city farms welcome visitors. This is in stark contrast to real farms, where no one looks forward to sportswear-draped families scaring the livestock or trampling the crops under impractically shod feet. Turn up at a real farm expecting to tickle the animals and enjoy a home-made scone and you will be as welcome as a turd in the thresher.

One argument in favour of city farmers presented by people who work at city farms – or 'hippies on benefits' – is that city farms help people from the inner cities – or 'chavs' – to better understand the countryside by pretending it exists in the middle of Bristol. Urban dwellers often lack a connection with the food they eat, but once they have visited a city farm they know that every Starburger or bucket of Popcorn Chicken they eat comes from an animal called Daisy or Henrietta who was happy right up until the moment she was dragged out of her field and slaughtered.

As well as allowing you to feed the fluffy animals who won't be killed in front of a crowd of terrified primary school children as they should be, city farms also allow you to look at the cows and pigs, enjoy a teacake, and even offer the chance to 'sponsor' one of the animals. But to anyone from the country, this idea is a confusing one. Unless you are a vegetarian, you already sponsor animals all the time. 'Raise this attractive, friendly animal,' you say to the farmer, 'and when you have killed it and cut it into bits that I can eat I'll give you some money for it.' Looked at in this light, the city farm doesn't offer much of a bargain: 'Raise this animal and as long as you never cut it up into anything anyone can eat I'll give you some money for it.' See?

THE BAKELITE MUSEUM
WILLITON, SOMERSET

If you like your thermoset phenol formaldehyde resin formed from an elimination reaction of phenol with formaldehyde, then you'll love the Bakelite Museum.

Set deep in the peaceful Somerset countryside and housed within a historic watermill which used to do less Bakelitey things, the Bakelite Museum is dedicated to everything about the first plastics to be made from synthetic compounds, and features everything you have always wanted to know about electrically non-conductive polyoxybenzylmethylenglycolanhydride.

The museum boasts one of the largest collections of vintage plastics in Britain, with exhibits from the inter-war period including hundreds of the domestic items that people now in old or middle-age were once glad to see the back of.

A Disneyland for lovers of phenolic resins, those who wish to commemorate their visit can also choose from the range of exclusive Bakelite-themed postcards (not actually printed on Bakelite), while those who have completely lost touch with reality can choose to stay overnight at one of the museum's range of pod caravans. Which aren't made of Bakelite, before you ask.

THE BEAUFORT HUNT
WILTSHIRE

A thoroughly awful day out not because of the cruelty to animals, but because of the people you will have to mix with. Some of the worst kind of desperate betweeded social climbers queue up to join the Beaufort Hunt purely because there's a chance — a tiny, weeny, itsy-bitsy chance that makes winning the National Lottery look like a dead cert — that Prince Charles will come along and kill something fluffy and squeaky. If it were Prince Philip who rocked up, there would definitely be something killed, even if it was one of the hounds that walked 'a bit foreign' or looked at him with slitty eyes or something.

You don't even need to be part of the hunt to be part of it. You can, if you wish, follow it 'on foot' in a Range Rover at 90 miles per hour to watch the fox get torn limb from furry limb.

Some townies will tell you that the fox is frightened by the whole thing. Balderdash — anyone who has seen the hunt knows that the fox is smiling all the way through and enjoys the exercise. If it thinks it is getting away it occasionally stops to let the hounds catch up. In return for this sportsfoxlike approach, the hounds rip it to shreds in seconds, just as it would have wanted.

Hunting undoubtedly plays an important part in rural society. It is a place for like-minded aristocrats to meet and get married — especially if they are already like-parented. And it is a great social leveller — whether you are the high-born son of a duke or simply the brother of an earl, you will find huntsmen the most welcoming, gentle people who kill animals for pleasure you could ever hope to meet. And they won't give two hoots if you went to Eton or Harrow, so long as it is one or the other.

But those country types, they won't take any hunting ban

lying down. 'Because if hunting ever gets really banned,' they point out, 'what will we do with all the horses and dogs we use? We will have no option but to hack them apart with a bread knife in the middle of the street and send your daughter the photographs. After that we might poison all the lakes, just to make the point. It's not our fault, it's yours.'

> **THE ENGLISH COUNTRY GENTLE-MAN GALLOPING AFTER A FOX – THE UNSPEAKABLE IN PURSUIT OF THE INEDIBLE.**
>
> Oscar Wilde on hunting.

CRAP DAYS OUT FROM THE RECENT PAST:
LAPLAND THEME PARKS

Britain's Lapland theme parks could be said to share a crucial flaw with all other Lapland Theme Parks around the world, bar one: they aren't in Lapland.

Lapland, of course, is where Father Christmas is from if you want to pretend he is real. In fact, it's pretty much all Lapland is famous for. Take away Father Christmas and you have a backwater of Finland marked only by its unusually high rates of alcoholism and suicide and a constant fear of Russia. Still, at least Lapland has regular snow, and reindeer, and sledges. Unlike Britain, which rarely has snow, and doesn't have reindeer, or sledges. Take snow, reindeer and sledges away from a Lapland theme park and you have nothing more than a department-store Santa's grotto. With no department store.

While most of Britain's Lapland theme parks are roughly equal in expensive failure, 'Lapland New Forest' on the Hampshire-Dorset border took the usual level of failure and gave it a Christmas bonus. Opened in November 2008, the park soon caught the attention of the British press when it was the subject of an impressive 1,300 complaints to trading standards from its 2,000-odd customers, who described it as 'a scam', a 'joke' and 'hell'. Ho ho no.

Depicted on its website as a festive winter wonderland, the park promised real log cabins, a nativity scene, huskies and a 'bustling Christmas market'. What it delivered were a closed ice rink, a picture of a nativity scene nailed to a wall, and some bored-looking elves smoking rollies by a shed. Just like the real ones do. In Lapland!

No one could have asked for a Christmas scene more depressing since the one where Herod was in charge of the games. But they got one anyway when, after queuing for four hours before being told to join another queue, one father finally lost his rag and actually punched Santa in the face in front of a group of small children. The incident was one of a number of similar violent episodes, including an elf being pushed into a pram, leading dozens of workers at the attraction to be pulled out for their own safety by an employment agency.

Even one of the site's bouncers, Adrian Wood, resigned from Lapland New Forest in protest at the crapness of this particular day out, telling the BBC he had been 'ashamed to work there', presumably before finding more respectable work at a lap-dancing club.

An attraction offering small children a chance to meet Santa and look at reindeer shouldn't really need bouncers in the first place, but when even they are quitting, you know you've done something really special. By mid-December enough people had heard about Lapland New Forest for it to have become popularly known as Crapland, and it shut down before Christmas. Unrepentant, director Victor Mears blamed the punters themselves, saying that the company closed the attraction because of 'intentional organised crowd manipulation and event sabotage', and is believed to have formed the world's first ever yuletide global conspiracy theory.

STANTON DREW STONE CIRCLES
SOMERSET

Many thousands of visitors to Stonehenge in Wiltshire go to marvel at prehistory's answer to the Millennium Dome and its surprising lack of size or inherent interest. Yet, astonishingly, few visitors are aware that in the nearby county of Somerset, Neolithic man built another, equally mysterious monument to disappointing bank holidays and unhappy children.

The Stanton Drew stone circles are a group of big stones so uninteresting that they aren't even on top of each other. That's right. A bunch of big stones which don't even merit the word 'henge'.

As if in apology for not having tried to balance a few on top of the others like those other guys did in Wiltshire, the Neolithic stone gatherers at Stanton Drew did, at least, offer an extra couple of circles for your visit. So it's a bit like your plumber saying he hasn't put in a bathroom as you wanted, but he has set up your DVD player instead and still wants paying.

The larger of the two rings, some 113m in diameter, is called the Great Circle. As if Stanton Drew's contribution to the putting stuff in circles community wasn't quite poor enough, not all of the big lumps are even there. According to archaeologists, the Great Circle probably originally consisted of 30 or more stones, of which just 27 survive today, and was surrounded by a ditch, which is now filled in. So at some point, someone came and took away three massive stones. For God's sake, why?

An attraction that could scarcely be crapper if it was made of wood. Imagine that, eh? Woodhenge.

WOODHENGE
DURRINGTON, WILTSHIRE

Just two miles to the north-east of Stonehenge, outside the village of Durrington, a monument exists that makes Stonehenge look like St Peter's in Rome. That monument is Woodhenge. That's right. Stonehenge on the cheap.

Woodhenge was 'saved' from obscurity in 1925 by Alexander Keiller, an amateur archaeologist and the millionaire inheritor of the Keiller family's Dundee Marmalade fortune, and his archaeologist friend OGS Crawford, who identified the site from an aerial photograph taken by a First World War air hero, Gilbert Stuart Martin Insall VC.

Yet while those making the discovery might have a pleasingly *Boy's Own* feel to their names, the site itself is far from King Solomon's Mines. Apart from anything else, all the wood has gone. Stonehenge, only made of wood, and missing all the wood. All that remains are circles of holes which probably had big wooden staves in them. Or maybe not.

Still, this was long before television, and Keiller and Crawford's discovery led to a full-on, three-year-long excavation of the site led by Maud Cunnington, a fellow archaeologist whose parents can only have chosen her name from a *Jeeves & Wooster* story. Had she been asked, Cunnington would probably have said something like: 'Woodhenge is a rich discovery of great historical interest that promises to significantly increase our knowledge of the pagan religious rites of Neolithic Britain, but I wouldn't visit on a bank holiday if I were you. Why not go for a walk in the countryside and stop in at a friendly pub?'

If you felt let down by Stonehenge or enraged by the Stanton Drew Stone Circles, Woodhenge will have you spitting blood.

ABBOTSBURY SWANNERY
DORSET

Love swans? Then you will like the Abbotsbury Swannery. But if you don't like swans, or only quite like swans, you probably won't like it as much.

> WHAT PASSES FOR COOKERY IN ENGLAND IS AN ABOMINATION... IT IS PUTTING CABBAGES IN WATER. IT IS ROASTING MEAT TILL IT IS LIKE LEATHER. IT IS CUTTING OFF DELICIOUS SKINS OF VEGETABLES... A WHOLE FRENCH FAMILY COULD LIVE ON WHAT AN ENGLISH COOK THROWS AWAY.
>
> Virginia Woolf, *To the Lighthouse*

SWIMMING WITH DOLPHINS
NEWQUAY, CORNWALL

Quite what the dolphins think of this whole farrago is anyone's guess. It seems a bit presumptuous to decide they have nothing better to do than tow what are essentially land-based animals around in the water. They have mackerel to catch for one thing. They don't expect us to give them a piggy-back around Coventry Cathedral if they fancy knocking about outside their natural environment. Just think how stupid you would look in a cathedral with a dolphin on your back. 'What's that, Jeff?' 'It's a dolphin on my back.' 'Thought it was.'

Swimming with dolphins makes as much sense as paddling with badgers or cooking with squirrels.

Despite this, people seem to think if they just leap out of a motorboat waving their arms like nobody's business and attempt to grab on to a passing sea-mammal's fin, the little chap will turn, smile kindly and ask where he wants to go, like an unusually smooth and wet taxi driver. They think that after a quick dip with a bottle-nosed dolphin all their deep-seated psychological issues will drift away in a sea of calm. Not a chance, sunshine. The dolphin will do his very best to drown you and that won't help you at all. It might well make things worse – nearly drowned by a dolphin, it doesn't sound positive.

Perhaps a clue that they are not 100 per cent behind the undertaking is the propensity of the squeaky hairless bastards to disappear as quickly as their fins will carry them at the first sight of some idiot in a wetsuit. And since there's a fair-to-middling chance that if that dolphin does let you get close to it, it's because it is actually a basking shark which could literally swallow you whole, you might just change your mind when you get close enough to realise just what you've done. Those stories you hear about dolphins protecting divers from shark attacks? Total propaganda. Any dolphin witnessing such an attack will do nothing but hang around on the sidelines watching and laughing as the stupid unwanted human gets what's coming to him for messing about in shark-infested waters.

There's a clue in the word 'infested'. Nothing 'infested' is nice. You don't get 'balloon-infested' parties. No one describes a summer as 'holiday-infested'. Sharks, they 'infest' like it's going out of fashion. Stay away from them and their snide dolphin mates.

And another thing, if dolphins are so clever how come:

a) They keep swimming into tuna nets

b) They haven't invented anything. Not even spoons.

Answer me that.

LONDON

MADAME TUSSAUDS
LONDON

By rights, spending £25 for an hour of looking at shop dummies dressed as quite famous people should be the sort of thing you do when you have exhausted every – *every* – other activity on the planet. And yet the queues for Madame Tussauds are longer than those that turned out to praise Chairman Mao on his birthday when he was in an especially genocidal frame of mind. There are people queuing for Madame Tussauds who have forgotten what they are queuing for and are only aware of a distant Zen-like goal, which eventually turns out to be giving the camera a smiling thumbs-up next to Hitler. It is actually the most popular tourist attraction in Britain, a fact which surprises for even longer than it makes you weep.

Madame T began her trade during the French Revolution making death masks of those just guillotined. The families wanted something to remember their loved ones by, and nothing says 'happy memories' like a wax impression of dad screaming in terror as a massive steel blade comes down to sever his neck.

What is most inexplicable is its popularity with people under the age of 18 who bounce off the walls fuelled by six litres of fizzy pop. For this, a generation – roughly 90 per cent of whom are clinically obese – manage to drag themselves from their reinforced beds. They even forgo their habit of surfing for hardcore Russian porn for which they set aside three hours of 'me time' each night. And you know how important that is to them.

So it remains a mystery: children who grow up dreaming of bustin' a cap in some pig's ass as part of their daily duties as a crack dealer and pimp, are excited by what amounts to giant novelty candles in one of the few places where a slow-burning fire would be welcome.

66

[NEW YORK] SEEMED SECURE AND WELL-DRESSED AS THOUGH IT WAS CONTINUALLY GOING OUT TO GAY PARTIES, WHILE LONDON HAD TO STAY AT HOME AND DO THE HOUSEWORK

Noël Coward

99

CRAP DAYS OUT FROM FROM HISTORY:
CLASSICAL THEATRE

After a hard day conquering Asia Minor, the Greeks liked nothing better than to kick back with a really intense five-hour play about incest and incest-inspired self-mutilation. Who wouldn't? It's a great way to relax.

The Romans, also keen on a long campaign or two, caught wind of this new leisure activity and added a bit of extra sauce here or there, but essentially kept to the tried and tested formula of really long days watching incest and self-mutilation. Nero himself was a keen amateur actor, singer and lyre-man, a bit like Michael Ball. His theatrical performances were so excruciating that members of the audience were known to feign death in order to be removed from the arena – still like Michael Ball. Nero also staged plays in which he would rape members of the cast at random while dressed as a horse, bear or bull – again like Michael Ball.*

_____

* For legal reasons, we must point out that this is really not at all like Michael Ball.

THE PRINCESS DIANA MEMORIAL FOUNTAIN
HYDE PARK
LONDON

Going to see water coming out of a pipe makes for a low-thrills day out wherever you are, but a trip to the Princess Diana Memorial Fountain is truly a dull exercise worthy of a princess.

This unique memorial to Diana, Princess of Hearts, 'aims to reflect Diana's life' and 'symbolises Diana's quality and openness' by being a fountain. All in all, it's just perfect for the family with a spare day and nothing else to do.

As Diana would have wanted – presuming she wanted to be remembered as a water feature – it was designed by American landscape artist Kathryn Gustafson and contains 545 pieces of Cornish granite lovingly shaped by the latest computer-controlled machinery in a factory somewhere.

'Water flows from the highest point as it cascades, swirls and bubbles before meeting in a calm pool at the bottom,' the Royal Parks authority guide informs would-be visitors. 'The water is constantly being refreshed, and is drawn from London's water table.' Unlike other London fountains, presumably, which are known to spit out weekly spouts of water drawn from a giant bottle of Perrier. And, just to point out the obvious, water always flows from the highest point to the bottom. That's just what it does whether or not you think you have trained it to do so.

The Princess Diana Memorial Fountain was turned on in July 2004. It was turned off again in July 2004, which is actually the same month. Things didn't get off to a great start when Elton John, one of the chief priests in Britain's Diana sinister death cult, described the fountain as 'hideous' and said it reminded him of a sewer. In the sense that both have water flowing through them and you wouldn't want to spend a day beside either, you can't fault his accuracy. However, the real problems began 24 hours later, when the fountain became blocked with leaves, which organisers discovered are quite common in London parks, apparently having something to do with trees.

Although the leaf problem was soon dealt with, using no more than a large team of people, by the end of July the fountain was closed again for safety reasons after three mourners managed to fall over in it and hurt themselves. This news left many wondering: How do you fall into a fountain? Are you walking towards it and forget to stop? Are you looking into it and miscalculate your angle of ascent? Are you in a black and white slapstick comedy and just couldn't help yourself?

Gustafson said she wanted the fountain to be accessible and to reflect Diana's 'inclusive' personality – words she must have regretted when the fountain was re-opened in August surrounded by a fence and six aggressive full-time security guards employed to stop the public from entering the water.

The problems continued. Although the weather was not particularly wet that month, seemingly the water in the fountain itself was just as wet as it always had been, and the grass next to it was swamped, meaning it turned into a memorial less of Britain's queen of hearts, more of its First World War dead.

To get around this, in December another alteration project was started involving removing the grass and replacing most of it with concrete. If the fountain could possibly have become less welcoming, it just had.

In all the project has cost £3.6m, which is arguably quite a lot for a fountain – B&Q is widely rumoured to do them for 50 quid – and it costs well over £100,000 a year to maintain. Which, I'm sure you'll agree, is money well spent on an upside-down tap surrounded by concrete, metal fences and guard dogs.

> **IN ENGLAND IT IS ENOUGH FOR A MAN TO TRY AND PRODUCE ANY SERIOUS, BEAUTIFUL WORK TO LOSE ALL HIS RIGHTS AS A CITIZEN.**
>
> Oscar Wilde

MIMEFEST
LONDON

FESTIVAL OF FOOLS
MUNCASTER CASTLE
LAKE DISTRICT

For at least a hundred years people have been trapping mimes in glass boxes, but still some of them have managed to get out, resulting in a complete lack of comedy wherever they go.

Whether they are not-hilariously walking into strong winds, or not-amusingly eating food, the laughs just never start whenever there's a mime about. Like a gathering of the BNP, you just can't enjoy life when there's one in sight.

And with the London International Mime Festival you can watch them go for a full week without so much as uttering a word or raising a smile. Why should we pay good money for an actor who doesn't say words? In the old days, actors would say words like there was no tomorrow and the audience would actually have a nice time. But not with a mime.

What's even worse than having to watch these white-faced, stripey-topped pretend-French bastards, is knowing just how seriously they take themselves. It's as if Jean-Paul Sartre had decided to put on a kids' show but flatly refused to talk during it and just kept staring at you.

A sample from the 2011 programme:

Flesh and Blood & Fish and Fowl: 'Convenience food firm middle manager Jerry pops out of a wheelie bin. But as tropical plants burst out of filing cabinets and wild animals take over the workplace, what starts as a parody of office politics and consumerism becomes a dark ecological satire. Mankind has lost the plot and the food chain is about to change.'

I'll tell you something, sunshine, someone has certainly lost the plot, and it's not mankind or the bloke in the wheelie bin.

Take your kids along to see 'a parody of office politics and consumerism that becomes a dark ecological satire' and they won't thank you. They wanted to see Bob the Builder.

Still, let's not judge the whole festival by one act. What about Les Antliaclastes: 'A micro comic-tragedy based on the cycles of the washing machine'. A washing machine. Why not a rug or a duster? Equally useful items but no better as a basis for a 90-minute show that costs £28. Try it for yourself: try sitting in front of your washing machine for 90 minutes and at the end of it throw £28 out the window to a passing French bloke who doesn't thank you. See how funny it is. If you don't have a washing machine, you can do it with any white good – a fridge, a cooker, a dishwasher – the ultimate effect is the same.

Then there's The Art of Dying: 'In 80 minutes of wordless comedy The Art of Dying explores the big taboo issue we all have to face but want to ignore. How does a clown die?' Strangely, it is an issue we do not have to face, and do not want to ignore. In fact, far from being a taboo subject, it is one we enjoy speaking of and openly discussing.

In 2010 the Telegraph said of Collectif Petit Travers, 'They can do things with balls that make your jaw drop,' and while we would not wish to contradict the Telegraph reviewer, we would suggest he rephrase this in the future.

After the performances, there are 'meet the artists' sessions, although the 'smack the artists' sessions would probably have been more popular.

A similar thing is on offer at the Muncaster Castle Festival of Fools, only this time they are close enough to touch you. And you know that they want to. For hour after hour jesters and stilt walkers amble about the grounds annoying people who came to see the castle and just want to go home again before the traffic gets too heavy. Really, once you have seen one man walking on sticks you have seen them all. But how long does the Festival of Fools last? Five days. Five!

It is a known fact that 80 per cent of mimes have been in prison for murder. According to this bloke we met in the pub.

"

A DULLER SPECTACLE THIS EARTH OF OURS HAS NOT TO SHOW THAN A RAINY SUNDAY IN LONDON

Thomas De Quincy

"

HARRY POTTER TOUR
PLATFORM 9¾, KING'S CROSS STATION
LONDON

Next up in the 'shameless cashing in' category is the Harry Potter Tour from the Carry On Tours.

'How do you fancy coming across Hagrid at Hogwarts, riding on the Hogwarts express and sitting down with Gryffindor students in the great hall?' reads the promotional literature. Well, we do, but since none of them exist even in the slightest, we know for a fact that if we hand our money over to you we are going to be disappointed. Indeed, all we do know is that Hagrid isn't here and we've blown £499. Rats' arses.

'Naturally, we'll be taking a ride on the Hogwarts express and even disembarking at Hogwarts station ...' But we won't be, because – and we really thought we had covered this – it's not real. Actually, we will be taking a ride on a train. You can do that for less than £499 any day of the week without booking. If you go on a local train and book well in advance, it can cost you as little as £2. That's £497 saved without even needing a railcard.

'First stop is Oxford where we visit Christchurch College and the famous Bodlein [sic] Library. Can you find any spell books?' Doubt it. They don't exist. Other things we won't be able to find include unicorns, square round things and tartan paint. Would you like us to waste our time searching for them too? We do have things to do, you know.

'Tonight we spend the night in the Peak District where if you're lucky we might find a village pub to discuss the day's events.' If you're lucky? You have to be lucky to find a pub in the whole of the Peak District? There are thousands of them. They advertise in the Yellow Pages. Where are these people taking you – some kind of Victorian Temperance League outpost? Will we roll up looking forward to a cheeky pint only to discover people round here tend to wind down with a glass of water and the Bible and hours of disapproving perusal of pornography? Not to mention that it's a bit suspect advertising trips to the pub for 11-year-olds. This isn't Sunderland.

Missing something of a trick, the tour doesn't start off from Platform 9¾ at King's Cross. Now the whole joke here is that Platform 9¾ doesn't actually exist. So when you follow the signs to get there, all you see is a blank wall with half a trolley sticking out of it. It's funny right up until the point when you realise your child is crying.

> **" A GHASTLY HEAP OF FERMENTING BRICK-WORK POURING AT POISON AT EVERY PORE."**
>
> John Ruskin on London

THE OXFORD AND CAMBRIDGE BOAT RACE
LONDON

The annual Boat Race between Oxford and Cambridge universities is pretty much the opposite of the Notting Hill Carnival; instead of upper-middle-class white people pretending to enjoy 'ethnic' things like steel drum bands, curried goat and being surrounded by mounted police, at the Boat Race lower-middle-class white people pretend to like posh things such as public schools, talking loudly about how much stuff they own and being rude to people serving them food. So for a day a substantial stretch of the river Thames is cleared of working-class people who might need to get to their jobs, in order that their social betters can skip merrily past in their pretty little boats.

Even more boring to watch than to take part in, rowing is officially the world's worst sport after golf. Unlike games such as football, which involve a modicum of strategy and skill, and require you to face the way you are going, the secret of success at rowing is simple: pull the oars, harder and more often. Maybe further. Actually we're out on a limb here and really just going by what we have seen on TV.

At ancient universities, though, rowers are apparently not a bright bunch, and require someone with a megaphone on the boat to remind them of this simple formula. Footballers are not Nobel Prize-winners either, but at least David Beckham never needed the coach to run around behind him screaming: 'Left leg forward! Right leg forward! Breathe, David, breathe.' Just in case he forgot the basic method.

Unlike other famous races, such as the Tour De France or London Marathon, which have scores of competitors, the Boat Race has just two teams. This means that after the three minutes it takes for the boats to pass your spot on the Thames, that's all the action over with. For a year.

If the Boat Race was sex, you'd grumble.

The fact that it is an entire competition made up of two teams, with no one else ever allowed to take part, also stacks the odds very much in the favour of each team coming in at least as runners-up, so no one ever has to explain to supporters why they are facing relegation.

The Boat Race is also an unlikely crowd-puller in that it is a competition between teams from two universities, not countries or cities. This means that most of those turning up have no reason to support either side. However, spectators care about the outcome for two reasons. The first is that their uncle George was really good friends with a chap whose wife's brother went to Oxford, and uncle George was easily their favourite uncle, or in their top three favourite uncles at least. Perhaps he was fourth. Actually, his name might have been Gerald.

The second is the belief that having a stake in the success of one of Europe's finest universities suggests to onlookers that while you didn't actually go to Oxford or Cambridge, you're comfortable in those circles, and you really might as well have gone to one of the two universities even if you didn't, you know, actually go to one of them. Perhaps you would have got in, if you had applied. And they had accepted your application. And you need to have an Oxbridge degree to know what that amounts to.

Allow us to explain: it amounts to automatic employment by the BBC in a creative capacity commissioning sports programming such as boat racing.

Those forced to spend the day watching the Boat Race can take one small consolation, however: Thames water is 27 per cent rat urine and occasionally the boats do sink. Sometimes they both sink – a 'golden day' as it is known in most circles.

SOMERSET HOUSE OUTDOOR CINEMA
LONDON

The outdoor film screening at London's Somerset House is inspired by the drive-in movie: an American phenomenon involving cuddling up to your wholesome sweetheart in an open-topped car to watch a film under the stars and hopefully smuggling your hand inside her sweater. After all, she did promise you.

Unlike America, Asia, Africa and southern Europe which can pretty much rely on good weather throughout the summer months, in London the only thing reliable about the weather is that it will disappoint you very much. This is the reason why you don't own an open-topped car, and also why you should just give up and leave the very second your sweetheart says: 'I think it's clearing up.'

One benefit of the outdoor film screening should be that it is cheaper than a screening at a normal cinema: after all, the organisers have saved on the cost of bricks. But in this respect the outdoor cinema is like employing cowboy builders: you don't get a proper roof or walls, but still end up paying twice as much as usual and your girlfriend mocks you when you fail to get your money back.

The Somerset House film screenings are all of 'cult' films. However, unlike real cult films, which are films that are strongly loved by a small number of die-hard fans, the cult films shown at Somerset House are films that are loved by a large number of people pretending to be die-hard fans.

The real appeal of the outdoor cinema experience is that the normal rules of the cinema don't apply. This means that unlike at the local Odeon, hard drinking is allowed – actually encouraged – so that the film soon becomes just a backdrop to a boozy picnic. This sounds excellent. However, unlike picnics, which take place in the country or at least in a park, Somerset House is in central London. This means that there isn't grass, just paving slabs, and instead of being filled with the sound of cheerful honey bees, the air is filled with the sound of furious cockneys, braying estate agents, trigger-happy armed police officers telling you to 'put the weapon down'.

> **LONDON, PRUDISH WITH ALL VICES IN EVIDENCE, EVERLASTING DRUNK IN SPITE OF LAWS AGAINST DRUNKENNESS.**
>
> Paul Verlaine

SHERLOCK HOLMES MUSEUM
LONDON

The first mystery at the Sherlock Holmes Museum is finding it. It is listed in all the guides as residing – quite naturally – at 221b Baker Street and one is quite impressed that the founders of the museum managed to secure the very rooms that the great detective resided in. Especially since he never existed. But when you follow your map and turn up at 221 Baker Street, you are a little concerned to find yourself staring at the grey concrete frontage of the Sun Alliance insurance company. 'Have they gone into literary nostalgia-based tourism as a sideline?' you ask yourself. 'Or have I just got the wrong street?' The answer is neither. The solution to this particular mystery is that the owners of the Sherlock Holmes Museum are somewhat factually inaccurate. The museum is not at 221b Baker Street; it is somewhere around 240 Baker Street and they have just put a questionable number on the front of it. Unless you happen to notice the unemployed actor who didn't get that job as Sweeney Todd at the London Dungeon standing outside the front door in a novelty Victorian policeman's cape, plastic helmet (circa 1980) and Nike trainers, you're going to turn around and head back to Pizza Hut. With hindsight, this might have been your best option.

But for those who do notice the geographically inaccurate entrance, and stump up £10, the door opens to a world of plastic novelty Victoriana. Heading up the stairs you will pass sepia-tinged photographs of horse-drawn carriages and, at the top, you are met by a be-whiskered and slightly rotund chap purporting to be Dr Watson. One feels that his attempts to engage anyone and everyone in conversation can only stem from the gnawing insanity resulting from boredom. Like a character in one of Conan Doyle's stories, his lips say little but his eyes scream 'Help me!'

Dotted around the room in which he sits are items best described as knick-knacks – the sort of thing you can pick up from a charity shop and which look quite old but you're not really sure what they are. You could spend a better and cheaper hour at an antiques shop. If the owners think any of the visitors are fooled by their haul from Oxfam, they are simply demented.

Elementary, my dear Watson? Balls, my dear Holmes.

But the true highlights of the 'museum' – four or five small rooms which act as little more than a precursor to the extensive gift shop which probably makes more dough – are the dummies wearing equally half-arsed Victorian dress supposedly representing scenes from Conan Doyle's tales. At least with Madame Tussauds at the end of the road, the dummies don't look like they have been nicked from the Help the Aged shop.

> **LONDON, THAT GREAT CESSPOOL INTO WHICH ALL THE LOUNGERS OF THE EMPIRE ARE IRRESISTIBLY DRAINED.** Arthur Conan Doyle

STRATFORD UPON THAMES
LONDONSHIRE

The town of Stratford-upon-Avon in Warwickshire attracts thousands of visitors each year due to the celebrity of its most famous son, William Shakespeare, who as a young man moved to London just as soon as he possibly could. But he moved nowhere near Stratford in east London, a carbuncle on the already unpleasant face of the London/Essex border that has been downmarket for the best part of 800 years and shows no sign of changing its mind.

Failure to grasp just which Stratford they should be paying their cheeky criminal cab driver £800 to take them to, leads to many hundreds of bemused American and Japanese families wandering the bleak streets of Stratford each year in search of Anne Hathaway's house, as immigrants from poorer nations hurry home to their tower blocks before night falls and the hoodies emerge, attracted by the smell of fried chicken and alcopops.

Since Stratford will be the centre of the London Olympics, its indigenous creature – the Feral Youth – will be the unofficial mascot of the British team and the first British person many a foreign visitor will come into contact with, so we can really show off our knife crime. Other aspects of traditional British life on display in Stratford will be the ever-popular Job Centre, the desolate street, and arson.

CRAP DAYS OUT FROM THE RECENT PAST:
THE CLERKENWELL HOUSE OF DETENTION
LONDON

This underground former prison might well have been the scene of the horrific mistreatment and neglect of nineteenth-century inmates, but it sounds more like somewhere you would have to sit and write lines after being caught sucking a Polo mint during geography.

> 66
> # LONDON IS A MODERN BABYLON.
> Benjamin Disraeli
> 99

PARLIAMENTARY DEBATES
LONDON

They say the two things you should never see being produced are sausages and laws. Both leave you feeling a bit sick.

No matter which party you voted for, no matter if you scrawled 'none of the above' across the ballot paper or turned it into a little paper aeroplane and launched it across the room in protest, you will always find some reserve of disappointment if you queue up to witness the public-school bunfight that passes for legislative process in this country.

The only thing missing to really complete the atmosphere is a first-year fag being tied to the fireplace with his trousers round his ankles – although it is not certain just how the Chief Whip really disciplines all those naughty, coquettish backbenchers.

A House of Commons debate is a strange mix of mumbling and cage fighting. Try to imagine Hulk Hogan and The Rock rowing over opt-out clauses from the forthcoming bill on subsidy reform rates under the wheat stock directive 4971a.

And so it continues, day-in, day-out, except for the occasional moment of sheepish silence when some self important MP has to mumble an apology for claiming the purchase of an entire town in Buckinghamshire on his expenses. For it was recently discovered to the shock and horror of no one except an ill-informed sheep in Wiltshire named Alan that MPs have a little habit of telling a few porkies on their expenses claims.

If you wander into the House of Lords – an Alzheimer's-confused stumble by Zimmer frame and bath chair through the corridors of Westminster – you end up staring at God's Waiting Room. Very little more than a sheltered accommodation for the elderly with Fascist leanings/parents, the House of Lords is a constant source of bemusement to tourists from other nations.

'Britain's a democracy, right?'

'Yes, the oldest major democracy in the world.'

'So these old men who look like they are dead – they were elected?'

'Oh no. That's what makes it a democracy.'

'What?'

Where the Commons is a rumble in Westminster, the Lords is a mumble in the care home. Slow, repetitive talking into the chest is the order of the day. And if anyone wants to interrupt the speaker, it usually means attracting the attention of his nurse – perhaps by shaking a little golden bell – who will then let off a few cannons and a Catherine wheel to bring her ward out of his happy little revel about when he was a boy and met Baden-Powell. Or Moses.

CRAP DAYS OUT FROM HISTORY:
ANYTHING INVOLVING MINSTRELS

That weird whiny music? Who could ever have liked it? Even Henry VIII put together something quite nice in 'Greensleeves' and he was the sodding king at the time so he had hardly any opportunity to play about on a Bontempi.

Before the Renaissance, minstrels (not the modern, chocolate type) tended to hang around on minstrel galleries, hoping someone would start a medieval-themed evening. Or an 'evening' as they would have called it back then. At that point, they would strike up with the music. They were on galleries to make it more difficult for people to hit them.

The minstrels playing would be the sign for the king to set the dogs on them and tell them to shut up or he would have them all beheaded and he couldn't hear himself think. Jesus. The little bastards. At this point the minstrels would stop playing again and huddle together for warmth and protection, hoping the king would get so mortally smashed he wouldn't notice if they struck up again with 'Gawain's latest' – a merry little ditty that would really set your teeth on edge with his trademark whiny stuff and the occasional boring thump of a loose drum. 'Sounds great, Gawain. Really whiny,' they would say. 'Thanks Robin. I tried to make it extra whiny this time. I thought it would really push people to the limit, tension-wise.' 'You haven't disappointed.'

Also, jesters were rubbish.

IDEAL HOME SHOW
LONDON

Plugged by Visit England as a genuine reason to come to the country, the Ideal Home Show is an enigmatically popular annual event. ('Hey Brad! Let's go to England, we can pay to enter a massive room stuffed to the rafters with crap we can buy over here and don't!' 'What's that honey? We can buy crap in England too? I was looking for a reason to go there and the whole thing about rich history, culture and beautiful countryside just didn't have me convinced.')

Let's cut to the chase. The Ideal Home Show is a big shop full of homewares. We are talking kettles here – actual kettles – the type you probably already have in your home. We're not knocking them, but they just aren't the stuff of dreams. In other words, it is like a giant Argos, except that your visit lasts all day and you have to pay to get in.

Unhappy husbands dragged along to look at options in spoons are regularly left speechless at the sheer bravado of their wives' insistence that it will be fun to spend the day there. In reality, for most heterosexual males it holds as much interest as *Dancing on Ice* or cupping another man's balls in his hand.

And doesn't its official sanction from Visit England mean that we are saying to the world: 'Yes, we nurtured Shakespeare, Bacon, Nelson and the Venerable Bede, but what we are really proud of, what we really think will swing it for you, is the chance to come over and buy a food mixer which you will take back home with you only to discover it works on a different type of electricity'?

For that matter, has no one attending the event stopped to ask why, if they need something, they don't already have it? If it really is essential – as everything, including newspaper supplements on fibre-optic Bolivian wine storage systems, claims to be these days – how come they are still alive? How come they haven't actually disappeared in a puff of smoke or been swallowed up by the unforgiving earth?

> **HELL IS A CITY MUCH LIKE LONDON.**
>
> Percy Bysshe Shelley

CRAP DAYS OUT FROM HISTORY:
VICTORIAN CHRISTMAS DAY

There was a lot of religion about in the Victorian era and unless you wanted to go to HELL you had to go in for it with all guns blazing. So while today's eight-year-olds look forward to unwrapping the latest violent computer game at 4am on 25 December, the children of yesteryore were dreading 18 unheated hours on pews with a sexually repressed fascist screaming bloody murder at them and forcing them to repent and describe – in great detail – their most sinful secrets.

Bible readings were the highlight of the day, and they were just as interesting, socially relevant and enjoyable to a nineteenth-century seven-year-old as they are to today's.

Yes, the Victorians loved to celebrate the birth of The Saviour by scaring the living shit out of kids. This is, of course, perfectly understandable to anyone who has met a child. Frankly, the more scared they are the better – they are less likely to happy slap you and film it on a mobile phone. But the Victorian child knew his place. It was in church, very, very worried.

Then home to the next highlight of the day: standing around a piano singing hymns while father sternly decided which child was most deserving of an extra holy beating in order to show Jesus's love for all humanity (except for foreigners). Each child hoping it would be them.

This is not to say Victorian children didn't receive any presents. Oh no. So long as they refrained from self-pollution for a full year and learned the middle names of all the kings and queens in sequence, they would get a small, dry tangerine in their stocking. And they would be thankful. After eating, the peel could be played with, making it two gifts in one. It could be a hat for instance.

And then, to bed, whimpering softly, while father put on his top hat and opera cloak, took his 'special' black bag in hand, and went out to look for fallen women who needed 'saving'. From him.

" **BAH, HUMBUG!**

Charles Dickens, *A Christmas Carol*

"

THE GEFFRYE MUSEUM
LONDON

The Geffrye Museum in London's painfully silly Shoreditch is the sort of museum that gives the south a bad name among northerners by charting the style of English middle-class living rooms. A sort of Ideal Home Show Through The Ages, it houses a collection of furniture, textiles, paintings and decorative arts that are displayed in a series of period rooms themed from 1600 to the present day. If all this sounds ever so slightly metrosexual, the museum's plans for celebrating the 2012 Olympics are like being trapped in a nightmare the *Daily Express* is having.

The Geffrye is a key partner in the Stories of the World: London event, to be 'a UK cultural celebration of diversity and creativity which will explore the stories behind museum collections and work with young people to create exhibitions and events around specific themes that will attract new audiences', and to be 'a UK cultural celebration of diversity' through 'intensive community and youth engagement work'.

The Geffrye's politically correct curators will also 'explore how other cultures have shaped our personal spaces, and examine the ideas about what makes a home and the way we live'.

If a day out spent looking at old living rooms wasn't bad enough, the prospect of being locked in a room with a bunch of people who think the *Guardian* is right wing, discussing cushions with local kids, will have you wishing you could have spent the day watching some bear-baiting or a public hanging. If London mayor Boris Johnson had any kind of balls, he would bulldoze the whole girly enterprise in favour of London's first Monster Truck Arena.

THE TURNER PRIZE
TATE BRITAIN
LONDON

If you fancy a bit of Tracey Emin, the Turner Prize show is definitely the place to go, we don't mind telling you.

But high-class totty like Tracey aside, you could well be forgiven for thinking the annual Turner Prize is awarded for the most ridiculous thing you can slap the label 'art' on. And no one has yet realised that when French weirdo Marcel Duchamp exhibited a urinal and called it art wayyyyyy back in 1917, he was actually making fun of people who would accept it as such.

Nowadays if Damien Hirst exhibited the contents of his paper recycling bin it would win the prize and Charles Saatchi would sell it for a billion pounds.

Previous Turner winners include the 2001 recipient Martin Creed's The Lights Going On And Off. And yes, that's what it was – the lights in a room going on and off. He didn't even spell the name in an interesting way or try to colour in the letters like a real artist would. Very slight excitement at the time was caused by some other 'artist' attempting to gain attention by throwing eggs at the walls. And also by Madonna, who was presenting the award (Christ alone knows why she was doing it), saying 'motherfucker' as she handed over the prize.

The next year Culture Minister (and former art student) Kim Howells pinned a statement to a board in a room designated for visitors' comments, saying: 'If this is the best British artists can produce then British art is lost. It is cold, mechanical, conceptual bullshit. Kim Howells. P.S. The attempts at conceptualisation are particularly pathetic and symptomatic of a lack of conviction.' Which was astonishingly honest for a politician. What next? David Cameron saying sometimes he looks at his mum and thinks: 'Nice tits!'

If you do attend a showing you will be up against an astonishing array of idiots competing to the death to see who can make the most nonsensical statement about something rubbish, in the hope that they will then be asked to write a column in the *Guardian*. Because at that point they can feel they have finally made it since the people they want to be friends with will no longer pretend not to see them in bars. Members of the public who are indirectly paying for this fiasco with their taxes, however, press their faces to the windows and look on in utter bewilderment.

In the old days, art galleries were filled with pictures that looked like things. Now they are filled with tossers. It's not a joke, it's just annoying.

> THE HISTORY OF MODERN ART IS ALSO THE HISTORY OF THE PROGRESSIVE LOSS OF ART'S AUDIENCE. ART HAS INCREASINGLY BECOME THE CONCERN OF THE ARTIST AND THE BAFFLEMENT OF THE PUBLIC.
>
> Paul Gauguin

SING-A-LONG-A-SOUND-OF-MUSIC
PRINCE CHARLES CINEMA
LONDON

The world tends to divide neatly into two types of people: Those who like dressing as nuns; and those who are having nun of it.

For the latter group, there are many leisure activities available: reading periodicals about historical research, weekends away in the Cotswolds, and playing squash with chaps named Roger are just three.

But for those who are more nun-based in their interests, Sing-A-Long-A-Sound-Of-Music presents ample opportunity to really let things rip. It's not a bad gig if you're into Nazis, too.

The audience to this monthly event – which sees the film screened while a compère somehow gets the audience to sing along, albeit with less joy than a boys' school choir in a rough inner city – splits into sections.

First there are the young women who are staggeringly into it. Wearing wimples and habits and necking Bacardi Breezers (known in the licensed drinks trade as 'nun fuel').

The males in attendance tend to be those who quite like dressing as nuns anyway, or those who quite like dressing as Nazis. Some of them favour a half-and-half option to get the best of both worlds – wimple on the top, jackboots on the bottom. The opportunities this provides for striking up conversations in Soho at 2am should not be underestimated.

In December you should also watch out for the work Christmas parties where men in suits are utterly horrified at having been talked into this by the 'wacky' secretary who will be sacked at 9am on Monday. And it's really not worth her while asking for a reference.

EEL, PIE AND MASH SHOPS
LONDON

Ever since the Krays started killing people for no good reason in the 1960s★, fashionable society has just loved Cockneys. And so London media types wearing square black glasses and purple leggings occasionally leave their Soho offices to venture into the East End to mix with 'real' people who 'really' want to stab them. While they are there they often pretend to like working-class things such as football and beer. But if they want to go one step further, they attempt to delude themselves that they also enjoy eating jellied eels, and for that purpose stop off in an eel, pie and mash shop to grin as if they wouldn't rather be anywhere else in the world.

Jellied eels are so vile it is a wonder society has not collapsed – men, women and children just standing in the street all day scraping their tongues with brass polish and mumbling. Lovingly encased in cold, salty jelly, the black rubbery body that seems still to be alive initially repels attempts to bite into it. And when you finally pluck up the courage and your teeth sink in, what's that? Oh it's the spine that you have to crunch through before attempting to swallow, while a little tear gathers in the corner of your eye. Locals wouldn't touch them with a 19ft bargepole.

Eels are now an endangered species, thank Christ. So the imminent dearth of fish in our territorial waters has its upside.

★ Salt of the earth, they were, loved their mum and they would shake your hand after they brutally stabbed you and your family to death. To show there were no hard feelings.

CRAP DAYS OUT FROM THE RECENT PAST:
FUNLAND, THE TROCADERO CENTRE
LONDON

Ha Duken!
Yoga flame!
Spinning bird kick!

Sorry, it's just that we still can't get them out of our heads. But if you recognise those almost-words, and sometimes wake up in the night, sweating and murmuring them into your pillow, then you too may have known the evil lure of Funland in the Trocadero Centre.

I know what you're thinking, reader: there must be some mistake. For how can Funland be a crap day out when it has fun in its very name? Yet by some strange mix-up of fate, Funland was in fact a highly depressing experience.

Located beside Piccadilly Circus, the Trocadero was a paradise of tacky, unwholesome entertainment for the teenage boy, containing everything your parents didn't want you to do on a day out, bar crack and cottaging. If you wanted those you had to join the Scouts.

And nestled among the cinemas showing brainless action films starring European men who had yet to master 'the talking', the brightly lit fast food joints and the video arcade games was parenting's very nemesis: Street Fighter II.

Huddled around a machine even more advanced than a Commodore 64, 12-year-old boys could watch in awe as acned 15-year-olds employed dextrous 'special move' button combinations to beat other teenagers playing as Ryu the karate guy, Ken the US marine, E. Honda the sumo wrestler and a host of other ethnic stereotypes – including Dalsim, the surprisingly aggressive Indian yogi and possessor of the Yoga Flame! special move.

In the neon gloom of the video arcade, where sunlight was banished and the concept of night and day seemed strangely remote, the minutes turned to hours and the hours to days as the innocence and freshness of youth faded.

Long school holidays were spent becoming thinner in the Trocadero's gloomy netherworld, drifting like a lonely, pale ghost yet strangely drawn to the transient glory of being that day's champion, which would allow you half an hour of grudging respect from your peers. Time was punctuated only by the occasional mugging by an older teenager short of 50p coins, or by the realisation that Christmas had come and you had to spend at least a day with your family. A long, boring day when your fingers tap-tap-tapped on the table and every sound could have been an Indian yogi about to perform Yoga Flame! on your mum.

The Trocadero was dark, unhealthy and soulless, and unlike a trip to a museum, a site of archaeological interest or the theatre, it was a terrible day out for which your parents could not, for once, be entirely blamed.

Yet with the advent of the video console, adolescent boys could develop thumb blisters from the comfort of their own homes, and the Trocadero had been stripped of its evil power at last.

Game Over.

GLOBE THEATRE
LONDON

Also known as 'ShakespeareDisney', the Globe is far and away the best place in London to see a play interrupted by aircraft noise. For anyone who likes plane-spotting, dislikes plays and really fancies standing for four hours in the numbing cold while nearby schoolchildren broadcast Snoop Dogg hustlin' bitches on their phones, it's a practically unrivalled experience.

The Globe attempts to recreate the Elizabethan play experience – right down to the things we have got rid of because they made everything much worse. Four hundred years ago, when you might have been sitting next to a plague-addled peasant, the fact that the theatre was open-air would have been quite welcome – and that vegetable smell which followed people around would have somewhere to drift to. But now the lack of a roof just means that when it rains, like in the song by Scottish novelty indie-lite chancers Travis, it always rains on you. Especially disappointed are the bewildered Japanese tourists who thought they had booked for *Cats*. They presumed it would include cats. And a roof. They spend most of their time pointing up and talking excitedly in worried tones.

Besides, if you really wanted to recreate an authentic Elizabethan play experience, you could do far more than just missing out the seats and allowing the weather to torment you. For a start, you could allow prostitutes into the audience to ply their trade then and there.

Just to return to the lack of the ceiling at the Globe – because we're not quite finished: the people who built the Globe – what do their houses have on top of them? That's right, roofs. We have the bricks, we have the wood, we even have the scaffolding, so come on Britain, what's wrong with roofs these days? And seats? Comfy seats – that's all we ask. Nice ones. Where you can have a snooze during the boring bits. And cake. We like Victoria sponges.

Something is rotten in the borough of Southwark.

WIMBLEDON LAWN TENNIS CLUB TOUR
LONDON

Now let's be clear: this isn't a rant about going to Wimbledon to see the tennis. No, going to see a professional tennis match while Cliff Richard warms up in the background 'just in case', is a perfectly decent day out. No, this rant is about going to Wimbledon when the tennis isn't on.

Yes, a trip to Wimbledon Lawn Tennis Club offers the chance to see those rectangles of well-kept grass and enormous stands live, empty, and at the very end of the popular District Line underground service. After all, it is the seating arrangements that people love so much about Wimbledon.

As well as grass and lots of empty seats, however, since 2006 Wimbledon has also boasted the Wimbledon Lawn Tennis Museum, an attraction that makes two initially promising serves but immediately faults on both to the disappointment of the crowd.

The first is a walking, talking hologram recreation of headband-sporting, umpire-hating, three-time men's singles champion John McEnroe.

Still perhaps the most famous name in tennis, the chance to see the Big Mac in all his brattish glory is something worth buying a Zone 4 one-day travelcard for. As any fool could tell you, the point of any John McEnroe hologram is to see him having a hissy fit and shouting 'you can NOT be serious' a lot at an entirely innocent man who has never before come across an American. But instead the investment is wasted in the form of McEnroe reincarnated to give you a tour of the Dressing Room. Here he narrates his yawnsome memories of the room which, like the stands, is an aspect of the club that is undoubtedly necessary but of no great interest in its own right. Then the

McHologran attempts to thrill you with tales of how he first met Jimmy Connors and other distinctly second-fiddle anecdotes. He might as well tell you about his pension arrangements.

The other, equally promising main feature of the museum is its impressive 200-degree cinema, which shows movies made on a special panoramic rig that used five cameras to produce action scenes that can be frozen and rotated around the field of action at any time.

Needless to say, 200-degree cinemas are few and far between but, alas, the technology is wasted on a film about the 'science of tennis', instead of being used properly to show car chases from *The Dukes of Hazzard*, Evel Knievel jumping buses and the scene from *Under Siege* in which *Baywatch* babe and Miss July 1989 Erika Eleniak emerges topless from a giant cake.

Just like watching Tim Henman, then, the Wimbledon museum gets your hopes up only to inevitably fall apart in the quarter finals leaving everyone wondering when the next train home is.

Its other attempts to entertain are unseeded entrants that don't make it past the first round, most notably the 'Whites of Wimbledon' exhibition of clothing that contains such objects of interest as Rafael Nadal's dri-fit 'pirate' trousers (no, us neither).

THE CLOWNS' CHURCH SERVICE
LONDON

SHOWZAM CIRCUS FESTIVAL
BLACKPOOL

In 2006, the Bestival on the Isle of Wight had to cancel a request that people come dressed as clowns. The reason? An apparently abnormally high rate of coulrophobia – fear of clowns – among its fans. Rubbish. No one is really afraid of clowns (apart from Insane Clown Posse, who are insane). Many people despise clowns, but that's not the same thing at all.

In order to deal with this terrible made-up disease, Blackpool's annual Showzam Circus Festival even runs pre-show encounter sessions to see you through the ordeal of watching men not being funny with buckets of confetti. Almost as if it were a real problem.

But if you really are afraid of clowns who are neither insane nor in a posse, then avoid the annual Clowns' Church Service; because there are shitloads of them running around. At no point in any holy book that we are aware of does God invite 'a busload of sodding clowns' into his home on the first Sunday of February in the Holy Trinity church in Dalston. This doesn't stop them turning up regular as clockwork, though. And how do they arrive? No, not in amusing cars with the wheels falling off, but in normal cars with wheels that don't fall off. Many of them come by taxi. That's not even trying.

The annual service has been running since 1946, but it was only in 1967 that the clowns were allowed to come in their costumes. Prior to that it was the world's most half-hearted clown show, where they stood about in jeans and normal shirts occasionally muttering. Plain-clothes clowns.

The choice of Dalston is an odd one. Not so much known

for clowns as for shops on their last legs and fried-chicken bars that appear to have closed down months ago but still have people eating in them and growling at passers-by, the area would be far better suited to an annual church service for car thieves; so long as the vicar doesn't plan to drive home. Well, he can plan all he wants; he's not going anywhere.

So what gives clowns the right to their own church service? They don't demand their own hospitals or clown garages, or shops specialising in enormous shoes. In fact, while we don't want to sound clownist, do Christianity and Clownism really go? It just seems that trying to drown each other in the font, pretending to eat the Bible and continually squirting the increasingly irate priest with a buttonhole flower are at least on the very edge of acceptable behaviour within a church.

An annual army regimental service? That sounds fine. A monthly bus drivers' communion? Sure, why not? A weekly Church of England employees' service? It almost goes without saying. But clowns?

> ## "THE GREAT WEN.
> William Cobbett on London"

ABBAWORLD
LONDON AND SYDNEY

ABBAworld is currently available to make you feel awkward in both London and Sydney, making it the world's first dual-hemisphere shame. You can visit one, then hop on a plane for 24 hours only to stagger into the other, cursing what seemed like a funny idea when you booked the tickets.

Now just to make things clear: we're not actually knocking ABBA. A bit of camp pop never did anyone any harm – as the 20 million supposedly butch hard-drinking Australians who own an album by the foxy/bearded foursome will tell you.

('G'day Bruce. You've strangled another crocodile, I see.' 'That's right, Bruce. I did it to the sound of *Dancing Queen,* followed by *Gimme Gimme Gimme (A Man After Midnight).* I find the messages they contain uplifting and empowering to my feminine side.' 'Righto.')

You will be pleased and surprised to hear that there is a gift shop where you can buy endless – and we really do mean endless – ABBA merchandise. If you ABBA-want-it, they will ABBA-get-it-for-you; so long as you can ABBA-pay-for-it.

Out of interest, what would an ABBA world look like? Obviously it would be quite colourful, with blue velvet flares something of a speciality for the ladies, and silver open-chested shirts for the gentlemen. Not unlike the East German pornography of the early 1980s.

LONDON COMIC CON
LONDON

Britain's annual convention of men who have never had a girlfriend and are unlikely to hit a lucky streak any time soon, is quite a sight to behold. Attended by people who dress up as Ferengi from *Star Trek*, the conference is a bit like a freak show in reverse: here the audience seem like alleyways branching off Evolution Street and it is the paid celebrity guests who look like normal people who won't try to drug your food then take photographs of you while you are unconscious. Well, there might be the odd actor from *Blake's 7* or *The Day of the Triffids* who looks like they would, but they are the exception that proves the rule.

If you look around you will be sure to spot many faces from TV – mostly *Crimewatch*, *Plumbers From Hell* and that Channel Five documentary about people with Obsessive Compulsive Disorder – but also a few star guests who tend to be experiencing what you might describe as a 'down-swing' of their careers: some *Tripods* veterans, an X-wing pilot or two, or even some bloke who donned a latex suit to play a monster from *Doctor Who*. Rumour has it that a certain *Star Wars* character will give you an autographed photo for a packet of ready salted crisps and a can of Dr Pepper.

HARRODS
LONDON

Walking around Harrods is a lot like walking around a large department store in London. In fact, you would be hard pressed to tell the two experiences apart.

It's hard to say just when – or how or why – looking at quite expensive clothes you don't intend to buy or food you can't afford to eat became a leisure activity in its own right, but somehow it ended up on the 'to do' list for foreign tourists in London. Which was lucky for Harrods and its former owner, Mohamed al Fayed, as British toffs had long since deserted the shop.

In fact some of the designer clothes in the menswear section are available in Debenhams; the Bendicks chocolates in the food hall are also on the shelves at Tesco; and the milk is pretty much the same white stuff you get at a BP garage at 1am as you avoid the peckish students paying for a Twix with a credit card. Still, what Harrods lacks in British pounds, it makes up for in petro-dollars.

From the Egyptian Hall with its fake mummies to the waxwork of Fayed himself situated among the men's underwear to scare the living crap out of shoplifters (you have to wonder who woke up one morning and decided that the one thing the men's pants section was missing was a life-size dummy of Mohamed al Fayed), everything about this overgrown bazaar is about show. It has more empty sparkle to it than a feature-length episode of 'The Diamante Show' on QVC dipped in silver paint and lovingly blasted with the finest glitter. This doesn't mean you can't have an enjoyable time and a stylish shopping experience. You just can't have it here.

It is also home to two memorials to Dodi Fayed and his most famous squeeze, Princess Diana. Fans of the two can gaze not only on the last wine glass Diana ever drank from (out of respect, it hasn't been washed since, which is a bit unhygienic) but also a bronze statue entitled 'Innocent Victims', which depicts the two dancing beneath an albatross. And who wouldn't want to be remembered as dancing beneath an albatross? She was, after all, known as the Princess of hearts and albatrosses. They were known to follow her everywhere.

> ## "THE WHOLE THING RATHER GETS ON MY NERVES
> Oscar Wilde on London
> "

CRAP DAYS OUT FROM HISTORY:
THE MILLENNIUM NIGHT

Never in the field of human celebration has so much been expected by so many of something so rubbish. In London, tens of thousands of people lined the Thames, having been promised a 'River of Fire' and under the impression that somehow the boffins had found a way to set light to water. And people say that educational standards are falling. It would no doubt have surprised firemen up and down the land to realise that whenever they sprayed water onto a fire they were only making matters worse for themselves.

In the end, what the public were actually treated to turned out to be 10 boats along the river letting off fireworks. A bit like a marine version of your school bonfire-night display, only without the safety talk beforehand from your chemistry teacher. Or hotdogs. Or attempting to persuade your mate to hold the wrong end of a sparkler that had gone out.

At the same moment the Queen was doing her best not to look as miserable as a Norwegian fisherman and instead sported a face like a bulldog chewing a wasp while she held hands with Tony Blair to bad-temperedly sway vaguely in time to 'Auld Lang Syne' in the Millennium Dome. Thank Christ no one asked her to do the Hokey-Cokey. Apparently there were meant to be other party games but Prince Philip said something about Chinese Whispers that got the whole thing called off.

As for the Dome itself, don't get us wrong, we're actually big fans. It looks like (finally!) the aliens have landed in Greenwich. It's just that everything inside the thing was awful.

The massive flop that was the Dome actually had most commentators saying that this would be the low point of Blair's career as Prime Minister. How he must look back on that and laugh hysterically now.

BOROUGH MARKET
LONDON

Borough Market in London is one of the best places in London to buy a £12 loaf of bread. Characterised by 'authenticity', the market offers the chance to buy 'real' food from 'real' producers instead of the mass-produced 'factory food' from faceless supermarkets that the rest of us seem to eat and enjoy. It has handmade croissants sold by genuine French people and sausages knocked out by Spaniards on their own unhygienic smallholdings.

There is also stuff written in chalk on blackboards, all old-fashioned like, picturesque round cheeses and salamis, coffee beans in little paper packets, and sometimes the one from *Two Fat Ladies* that is still intermittently breathing. All the produce is made on small farms and all staff are middle-class farmers or cheery labourers from countries that middle-class people go to on holiday.

This distracts from the fact that Borough Market's 'traditional rustic fare' is as expensive as if it were fashioned by Michael Jackson. Far from realising what deluded idiots they have been for buying into London's olde worlde food theme park, however, most punters actually think they have 'discovered' it. But it is as likely an undiscovered gem as that statue of a disabled man in a sailor's hat that you stumbled across in Trafalgar Square.

OK, OK Mr *Guardian*: farmers do sometimes get shafted by supermarkets, which have too much power over the small producer blah blah blah. But paying a fiver for a piece of cheese the size of a mobile phone isn't sticking it to The Man; it's getting shafted by a yokel. Likewise, herbs and spices aren't frankincense or myrrh, you can get them in Lidl, and a Spaniard in London is about as rare as a Pole on a building site.

Borough Market isn't about authenticity, getting in touch with the land or standing up for the small producer – it's about paying double supermarket prices to have the small producer jump on your back and ride you, laughing with the in-bred farm hands as he thrashes your gullible buttocks with a crop.

THE EMIRATES STADIUM TOUR
LONDON

Let's face it: football is for thickos. Sure, Albert Camus might have played in goal a bit, but then he found everything so boring that his work is characterised by a pervasive sense of existential despair. And the fact that Frank Skinner and David Baddiel profess an interest in the game is only so they can get lucrative gigs like knocking out laughable World Cup singles and hosting that *Fantasy Football* show.

Anyway, all this is just a roundabout way of leading into one of London's least promising days out for anyone who can read without moving his lips: London's Emirates Stadium.

'Who do you support?' 'Emirates.' 'Who?' 'Sorry, I mean Arsenal.'

Yes, so commercial is the 'beautiful game' these days that the ground of one of England's top clubs isn't named after the team or its location, but after its sponsor, a Middle Eastern airline. That, of course, is old news to the club's polyester-clad fans, who flock to the ground when there is no match on for the chance to pay £15 to inspect the grass, sit in the bunker where the team's coach chews gum and buy that week's replica shirt.

Those not content with spending £15 on visiting a stadium where no one is playing can also invest on the 'Legends Tour', so they can be shown around by a player who can remember when the name of the ground didn't make you think of a Middle Eastern airline.

Players conducting the tour include 1970 European Fairs Cup final goal hero Eddie Kelly (remember him?); seventies FA Cup heroes Charlie George and Sammy Nelson and 1987 League Cup-winning captain Kenny Sansom, who offer carefully vetted thoughts on the current Arsenal team and what it's like living in a care home.

The Legends Tour, which costs a legendary £35, also comes with a signed photo of the Legend in question and an unspecified but definitely limited edition Legends Tour gift. It also offers the opportunity to spend £4 on Legendary souvenir programme 'The Spirit of Arsenal', which 'begins with an inside look into the modern state-of-the-art Emirates Stadium and then through the Club's fascinating past' – in other words, what you've just paid £35 to find out about already.

For football fans actually allergic to their own money, there is also the chance to spend a further £6 on a visit to the Arsenal Museum, where visitors can witness such sacred relics as Michael Thomas's boots from Anfield '89 and Charlie George's FA Cup Final shirt from 1971, along with an 'array of newly donated memorabilia' that seems to consist largely of football boots, shirts and medals. Which by our reckoning comes to a nice round £45 for the chance to see some grass, meet a bloke you've barely heard of and see someone's old gym kit. You see? Football is for thickos.

> "I LIKE THE ENGLISH. THEY HAVE THE MOST RIGID CODE OF IMMORALITY IN THE WORLD."
>
> Malcolm Bradbury

BUCKINGHAM PALACE TOUR
LONDON

Every year for a couple of months the people of Britain are allowed to queue for hours on end to get into the State Rooms of Buckingham Palace so that they can see what their taxes are paying for.

For this they pay merely another £20, which represents excellent value for money – after all, with most working adults already paying thousands of pounds a year to keep the rooms in pristine condition for the Queen, her rude husband and their developmentally challenged offspring, another £20 to actually make sure the cleaners meet the standards we are paying for, is money well spent. It would be so disappointing to pay all those taxes to make Elizabeth II – who has a net worth of around £500 million – comfortable, only to discover later that there was a pea under her 25th mattress. A bad night's sleep could really hamper her output of officially naming ships.

The State Rooms are full of the gifts the Queen has been given by the various heads of state who have visited her and her identically unemployed predecessors over the years. These are actually much like the glass unicorn and china doll-type bric-a-brac your nan keeps on her mantelpiece, only studded with platinum and encrusted with jewels the size of Wotsits. Also on show are fine works of furniture and porcelain. Of course, if they were to display the chamber pot used by George III – the actual one – most of us would be round like a shot to see it. Ditto ten-fold if we were allowed to view the very toilet that the Queen now uses. Which says what about us?

For no less than £65 you can have a guided tour of the place. For the extra £45 you are allowed to know what things are – for those on the second-class tickets it is all a secret, and if you ask you are met with a knowing smile and a gentle tapping of the side of the nose. For those who are really into it, there are 'unlimited admission' tickets, although if you try hopping over the wall at 2am carrying a crossbow, one suspects you will discover that 'unlimited' is not to be taken literally. There are, in fact, 'limits'.

And that's a pity because you do want to have a quick peek under the sofa just to make sure the 800-odd maids and domestic staff haven't missed a Chocolate Hob-Nob and the Queen has enough swans to eat. For, as every schoolboy knows, the Queen only eats swans, and every swan in the world belongs to her and she catches them with her bare hands whenever she is peckish. Many visitors to Buckingham Palace choose to extend their day out during the summer months by going down to Tower Bridge to watch the British monarch creep silently through the bull rushes, waiting with every sinew tensed until she spies her prey, at which point she leaps majestically from the undergrowth and breaks its neck with a single bite of her powerful jaws.

She wastes no time in eating her meal, sometimes swallowing it whole to the laughs and cheers of the crowd. This magnificent spectacle is all included in your £20 ticket.

All right, the last bit about the Queen being feral isn't entirely true. But it would be worth the money.

THE CHANGING OF THE QUILL
LONDON

Now that London has an elected mayor – at the time of this book's publication it is Boris Johnson, who really belongs in the *Beano* – the other mayor, the entirely separate Lord Mayor of London, who is chosen for his ceremonial post by rich people, is at a bit of a loss for stuff to do. He's had his big annual Parade and there's not much else in the diary apart from meeting bemused foreign businessmen who are surprised that some people dress like they are in a panto.

But every three years on 5 April his little eyes light up as he leaps out of nanny's bed and cries: 'Hello world! Today is the day of the Changing of the Quill!' And off he scampers to get dressed in his favourite big pirate's hat.

After his Coco Pops with extra sugar, he is driven to the Church of St Andrew Undershaft where he chats to a statue and ceremonially replaces the quill in its hand. Yes, a bleeding statue. No one knows what he chats about but he might be asking for advice on how to talk to girls, perhaps, or how to guarantee a soufflé will rise.

The statue is of John Stow, an unremarkable sixteenth-century historian who recorded social anecdotes about London life and sometimes made fun of cripples. The mayor then, barely able to contain his excitement, delivers an address to the model of a man from the waist up and changes the quill in the terracotta figure's hand. What he does with the old quill is not known but we suspect he keeps them all in a special box under his bed which is marked with 'Private! Keep out!' written in biro.

JACK THE RIPPER WALKS
WHITECHAPEL
LONDON

Has anyone who has gone on one of these trips stopped for a second to remark on the fact that they are giggling at the exploits of a man who ripped women's organs out for something to do on a Thursday evening? Just because it happened a century ago and they were whores – therefore not as important as, say, coke-head advertising executives but more important than office temps – it doesn't mean it didn't hurt them. If some go-getting young leisure industry entrepreneur from Yorkshire had the bright idea of a Yorkshire Ripper Walk, it's a fair bet that most people would think at least twice about booking tickets.

Even then, it's only about half an hour into the light-hearted walk about dead prozzies through the less-interesting parts of Whitechapel that you realise you're not even going to get the cheap thrill of seeing where the ladies got dead. Two World Wars and a hell of a lot of gentrification have demolished pretty much every building that Jack would have clapped eyes on. You can call in at the Ten Bells pub where one or two of the soon-to-be-mutilated got drunk enough that the unending night of their existence was put into soft focus, but the blood has all been washed away now and you don't even get a glimpse of a hooker. Pity. For that you have to spend £50 in one of the popular local brothels.

What you do get is pretty much a tour of the local mini-supermarkets that specialise in supplying cheap booze to the students stumbling up Brick Lane who are too poor, thanks to tuition fees and the soaring price of stupid clothing, even to buy half a pint of Cobra in one of the Bengali restaurants.

CRAP DAYS OUT COMING SOON:

THE OLYMPICS 2012 OPENING CEREMONY LONDON

Given that it hasn't happened yet, you might think we're being a bit negative with this one. You might think that we're just a bit pessimistic about things in general. You would be right, but in this case what we're actually being is realistic: the Olympics Opening Ceremony is always rubbish.

China's opening ceremony in 2008 might have been bigger, brasher and more partly-faked-using-CGI than many before it; but even that stuck to the usual format of gymnasts, dancers and themed choreography. Things as interesting to the average heterosexual adult male as baton twirling by other men. And Britain is less likely to use slave labour to make our version as gloriously successful.

However this is not the view of Jeremy Hunt, Secretary of State for Culture, Olympics, Media and Sport and James Blunt's main rival for a place in the cockney rhyming slang dictionary, who described the ceremony as 'the jewel in the crown of any Olympics and Paralympics and one of the benchmarks against which all games are judged'.

It's not though, is it? What people care about is the men's 100m sprint and the women's beach volleyball. And what they remember is how many runners are busted for downing half a pound of steroid tablets ten minutes before a race and then claiming that it must have been in the cold and flu medication they took in 2003.

So to make the opening ceremony a success, a crack team of 'creatives' has been chosen – after all, art is always best made by committee – led by film director Danny Boyle who is best known for the heroin-chic *Trainspotting* and the Zombies-silly *28 Days Later.* Junkie zombies – just the image Britain wants to project.

Boyle has so far been reticent about what shape the event will take. But clues for just how the opening ceremony might look could be found at the ceremony when Beijing handed over the Olympic flag to London. The event featured the urban dance group Zoo Nation – you know, Zoo Nation? – the world-famous disabled dance group.

The dancers were dressed as London commuters, waiting for a bus by a zebra crossing, before a double-decker bus drove around the stadium to music, before stopping and transforming into a privet hedge featuring London landmarks such as Tower Bridge, the Gherkin and the London Eye.

And just in case a bus that turns into a hedge full of landmarks might have seemed confusing, guitarist Jimmy Page and singer Leona Lewis then performed the Led Zeppelin song 'Whole Lotta Love', before David Beckham kicked a football into a crowd of athletes.

Another clue as to what the event might look like came from a blog post on the London 2012 website by Olympic collaborator and, er, Historic Royal Palaces' first very prestigious Artist in Residence, Rachel Gadsden. There is, Gadsden wrote, 'a clear indication that we do have a common sense of the human expression that is the Games. And if we can tap into this we will indeed contribute to a ceremony which will be capable of touching everyone. So we collaborate in a universal landscape where politics, religion and conflict play no part.'

Which should really clear things up.

THE ANAESTHESIA HERITAGE MUSEUM
LONDON

'Mum. Can we go to the Anaesthesia Heritage Museum? Pleeeeeeeease?!'

Words you will never hear. Never.

> **A VAST GRAVEYARD OF STILLED HOPES.**
>
> Ford Madox Ford on London

CRAP DAYS OUT COMING SOON:

THE QUEEN'S FUNERAL AND THE CORONATION OF KING CHARLES III

It can't be long now. Not with Charles setting off firecrackers under her chair every time they sit down for a meal and jumping out at her from behind doors wearing a hooded cloak and carrying a huge scythe. Frankly, it's a wonder she has lasted this long.

The rumour is he has tried it all: leaving roller skates at the top of the stairs, booby-trapping new supermarkets in case she opens them, rabid corgis. Charlie has pretty much tried everything during his Operation Royal Reaper. Sooner or later, he's going to hit the jackpot and from then on it will be his mush on the stamps. He will celebrate by making a plant Foreign Secretary.

But first we're going to have to get through his mum's funeral during which we will be forced to line the streets looking suicidal with grief whether we like it or not.

First there will be the national outpouring of shock. This will be triggered by the announcement through every medium known to man that a woman in her nineties has died. No one will believe it possible. They will only be convinced when police roam the streets breaking the windows of anyone not crying.

The funeral will be attended by the heads of all the nice states. Not invited will be the heads of all those who have previously described Britain as 'the Great Satan'. Many Commonwealth countries will volunteer to sink themselves out of respect, and pandas will cry.

And, without exception, we will all be part of it. If you want the police to do anything other than join in the next time you are being mugged, you had better turn up to wave off that royal coffin. Anyone not attempting to cut their own throats in grief is going to be suspect. You won't be safe until she's contemplating the daisies from the root end.

Then turn that frown upside down for Charlie's new job at the sprightly age of 70-something. His coronation will probably be a relatively low-key affair, with vegetables making up most of the guests. Although, unlike the funeral, your absence from the festivities will not be documented by the police's new Citizen Loyalty Investigation Militia, not eating a cream bun at one of the street parties will probably still get you shot by someone who lives nearby. For that reason, it would be best to buy the red, white and blue face paints before the shops run out.

But everyone loves a street party. The balloons twisted into the shape of the new monarch, meat pies in the shape of Camilla. It's a chance to get to know your neighbours and realise that you just can't stand them. Because hating them before meeting them would be prejudice. Hating them afterwards is just an informed decision.

THE SOUTH COAST

THE ISLE OF WIGHT GARLIC FESTIVAL

Do you know where kids love to go for a trip? Anywhere with the word 'Disney' in the name. Do you know where they are a bit lukewarm on? Anywhere with the words 'Isle of' in the name, or where the Archbishop of Canterbury might go on holiday.

It's a safe bet that the Isle of X is a great place for a) seeing flowers close up, b) banking, c) being flogged for homosexuality. Rarely do you hear children cry: 'Daddy, daddy, please can we deposit your salary in a tax-efficient super-capitalised vehicle! Pleeeeeease!' 'Oh, all right Jemima.'

So if you find yourself on the Isle of Wight you might find your mind drifting from thoughts of suicide through a haze of depression to the island's 'popular' Garlic Festival. Which is mostly about garlic and simply promises more fun than any pungent member of the alliaceae or onion family can deliver.

There are all sorts of garlic-related activities spread over a whole 48 hours. 'Arrive hungry!' screams the promotional literature. Presumably, you have to. 'Leave stinking!' it could add.

Musical entertainment is sometimes provided by The Wurzels – casting doubt on the widely accepted theory that they are dead. And it's not just garlic that's on offer: seasoning-based parliamentary democracy is part of the deal. Local MP Andrew Turner always takes a stall, explaining: 'I have taken a stand at the Festival as it is a useful opportunity to find out what local people are thinking.'

They are probably thinking, 'Why is my MP sitting here manning a stall about garlic?'

Of all the foodstuffs in the world, you do have to wonder why someone would pick garlic upon which to base an entire festival. It is, after all, known for sharply dividing opinion, and even causing close friends to fall out. Why not, say, chocolate?

Have you ever heard someone say: 'I'm not going near you tonight, you smell of chocolate'? Or 'Don't come near me with that delicious aroma of fine wine!'

The odd thing is, the Isle of Wight must be absolutely garlic crazy, given that one of its other chief attractions is The Garlic Farm, dedicated, not unreasonably, to 'all things garlic'. But surely 'all things garlic' is restricted to 'garlic' – there is nothing 'garlic' that is not garlic; isn't that the case? Or have we missed something? Maybe – we have been at this a long time, you know.

Sadly, once you have finished with the garlic-based activities on the Isle of Wight, you will find there is nothing left to do but go quietly mad.

THE WAY TO ENDURE SUMMER IN ENGLAND IS TO HAVE IT FRAMED AND GLAZED IN A COMFORTABLE ROOM.

Horace Walpole

COWES WEEK
ISLE OF WIGHT

Cowes Week really puts Cowes on the map. It doesn't put cows on the map – that would be absurd – but for seven days overweight posh men flock to this uninteresting port to pull giggly drunken blondes whose parents thought it not even worth the bother sending them to school.

Cowes Week was started in 1826 by George IV while he was ruling as Regent due to his dad, the sensibly named George III, being madder than a bagful of badgers. (He had a habit of addressing oak trees in the belief that they were the King of Prussia, which was considered a curious breach of convention.) George IV – a.k.a. Georgie Porgie Pudding'n'Pie – was an extraordinarily overfed man. His frame was virtually spherical and he would have been quite useful as a buoy, but managed to combine his non-traditional shape with a sexual appetite that could only be described as 'indulgent'. He therefore preferred to stay on land where he could harass female members of the aristocracy.

Annually rolling him down to Portsmouth and floating him across to the Isle of Wight seemed a good way to keep the younger daughters of unimportant earls safe for a few days each year, during which time they could either recuperate or attempt to flee the country.

These days Cowes Week has little more to do with sailing than Georgie had as he wobbled along the seafront in search of another ice cream. Plus, the Solent channel which separates Cowes from the mainland is so polluted that anyone falling in can probably walk to shore, which is a pity for more than one reason.

BRIGHTON BEACH VOLLEYBALL
SUSSEX

Like our nudist beaches, Britain's Knockabout beach volleyball contests bear testament to this nation's spirit of determination to ignore our weather.

As you may be aware, beach volleyball is a sport popular in places such as Rio de Janeiro, Hawaii and Los Angeles, and is characterised by shiny suntanned players and sun-kissed white sand. For all this country's many strengths, these are scenes about as likely here as seeing Stephen Hawking on *Gladiators*.

One of the Knockabout venues, Brighton beach, is actually so crap it doesn't even have sand, meaning that the organisers of the event had to cart in 200 tonnes of the stuff. But Brighton at least had the upper hand on the organisers of the Knockabout events in Cardiff, Glasgow and Milton Keynes, which don't even have beaches.

Brighton, in fact, is so determined to offer beach volleyball that it has set up the Yellowave centre, a permanent beach volleyball venue which also offers other sand-based versions of proper sports, such as beach soccer and beach rugby, as well as 'bouldering', a sort of low-key version of climbing in which participants go sideways instead of up.

As fans of football, cricket, rugby and tennis are aware, Britain has a long history of inventing sports, exporting them worldwide and then getting whipped at them for time eternal. For that reason, trying to import a game at which other countries are already good and for which we lack any of the crucial ingredients, might appear something of a questionable idea. However, it is, by contrast, a testament to the Briton's resolve and his have-a-go spirit of plucky amateurism.

Before our American readers start chuckling, they might also want to consider that – like baseball (i.e. rounders), basketball (i.e. netball) – beach volleyball is a girls' sport anyway and if you spent less time playing rugby in crash helmets and padding, you would be better at football.

"

I BEGIN ALREADY TO FEEL MY MORALS CORRUPTED.

Jane Austen on Brighton,
in a letter to her sister

"

GENESIS EXPO MUSEUM OF CREATIONISM
PORTSMOUTH

Yep, we have one. You never knew it existed, but there is a museum of Creationism in Britain. No one is quite sure why it's in Portsmouth, best known as a staging post for sailors to get a quick dose of the clap before they head out to sea, but there it is, standing proud. Just like one of those sailors.

Dedicated to proving Darwin was a tosser and probably in a gay relationship with Richard Dawkins, the Genesis Expo has oddly clashing exhibits. In one room they have a case correctly showing how DNA analysis proves all humans are descended from one man and one woman. In another they have an exhibit 'proving' that life cannot form from chemicals – such as DNA. It's a bit confusing.

There is also a slightly threatening gravestone with Darwin's image on it, although the fact that he keeled over 100 years ago probably means he's not too frightened. Some of the stuff is downright silly, such as the hourglass that 'proves' rock sediment can form in seconds because that's how long it takes for the sands to run down from one bell to the other.

But don't miss the 45-minute video that the Expo is proud to announce 'is played continuously'. They believe this is a selling point rather than one more black mark against them. An otherwise pretty video of little fishes under the sea, you are put off by the narrator constantly laughing at the idea – ha ha! What an idea! – that the different species could have evolved without the Almighty knocking them up in his workshop in a spare moment between llamas and alpacas.

In one sense the creators of the Genesis Expo have done the impossible, by creating a museum where you can come out knowing less than when you went in.

The visitors' comments book makes for fascinating reading:

'This is a fantastic museum and just shows how crazy Darwin's evolution idea is.'
But does it? Does it really? Is Darwin's evolution idea actually 'crazy' – i.e. is it actually suffering from an advanced state of mental illness – schizophrenia, psychotic paranoia, megalomania, for instance?

'It is great to see your witness – Creation is God's loudest message.'
Surely that was Led Zeppelin's 'Stairway to Heaven'… although Rolf Harris did a pretty good cover version.

'It was really interesting. Nice to have something like this in Portsmouth.'
Christ, is it? We have only been to Portsmouth once and it didn't seem so bad that a museum claiming men rode dinosaurs could improve the cultural life of the place.

'Excellent to find out more of how science backs the Christian story of Creation.'
You really have missed the point, haven't you? This place is essentially about how science is for gits and only those who ignore it will be laughing come Judgement Day.

'An amazing place – much needed. We are home educators from Windsor and come whenever visiting family in Bognor.'
For us, home education just became a very sticky subject. And so has Windsor. Bognor was already off the agenda.

'Absolutely brilliant! Will be suggesting to my boss we bring our clients here.'

It's your funeral. Unless it actually is a funeral, in which case we don't suppose your client will be in any fit state to care either way.

'Thank God someone is trying to tell the truth at last.'
Yes. All those satanic science-liars who are in on the big conspiracy. One day one of them will crack and let the velociraptor out of the bag.

'Very mind touching.'
That's not even English.

66

BUGGER BOGNOR.

George V's dying words, upon the suggestion that he could go to Bognor Regis to recuperate

99

CRAP DAYS OUT FROM THE RECENT PAST:

PLANET HASTINGS CRAZY GOLF (RIP)
HASTINGS

If the former seaside resort of Hastings in Kent could have become any more depressing, it did so in 2010, when the town suffered the loss of two of its best – well, only – known landmarks in the course of a month.

The first of these was its derelict pier, which after a suspected arson attack, burnt down in October that year in a fire that lasted for more than four days despite being surrounded by water on three sides and by sand on the other.

Less than a fortnight later, the second attraction to go was the Hastings Seafront Crazy Golf course, which saw its last round played on the 17th of the month. One of a chain of Crazy Golf courses originally set up by celebrated American golfer Arnold Palmer, the Hastings Seafront Crazy Golf course was said by the game's connoisseurs to have been one the finest courses in the UK with all of the other quirks that make crazy golf so crazy.

The game's local enthusiasts were thus distraught to hear that their beloved course was to be bulldozed in order to make way for an, um, Pirate Golf course. This was a humiliation for the town's Crazy Golf players, who have since been forced to undergo the indignity of having to putt the ball between the sails of a pirate galleon instead of a miniature windmill.

Planet Hastings was actually built on the site of the Hastings Model Village. In 2008 some of the model houses were uncovered during a bit of gardening, oddly making it the world's first and only model archaeological site.

CRAP DAYS OUT COMING SOON:
THE CRAZY GOLF MUSEUM

In the future, when we all ride about on jetpacks and hover boards with our alien pets, when our meals are downloaded from the internet and when the doctor's surgery no longer shuts for two hours in the middle of the working day, bored families will be able to spend a day out at Britain's Crazy Golf Museum.

This is the brainchild of Tim 'Ace Man' Davies, five-time World Crazy Golf Champion and co-author of seminal crazy golf history *Nutters with Putters* (order now for Christmas!), and Richard 'Squire' Gottfried.

The pair already have the honour of running the world's most visited websites and blogs on the irritating pastime, including the World's First Virtual Crazy Golf Museum – an online archive of miniature golf memories, histories and ephemera.

However, the pair's stated goal is to turn their virtual museum into a bricks-and-mortar attraction dedicated to proper golf's miniature, novelty cousin and which will be more difficult to avoid.

We just hope we live to see the day.

BOURNEMOUTH SEWAGE WORKS
DORSET

The Sewage Works at Bournemouth in Dorset combine two qualities rarely found in the same tourist attraction: being simultaneously boring and disgusting.

In 2009 the owner, Wessex Water, opened up the Bournemouth works to visitors as a celebration of its success in giving the seaside town some of the cleanest bathing water in the region – or as you might also put it, having successfully cut the crap.

A visit to the works offers an experience described in the company press release as 'an exciting, behind-the-scenes look at how dirty water is treated to a standard that is 100% compliant with EU mandatory standards'.

And if your lifelong dream is to see total compliance with EU standards live and in the flesh, the Bournemouth Sewage Works is the attraction you've been waiting for.

The most literal interpretation of a crap day out to be found in this book, the tour is conducted – for some reason that certainly escapes us – on a vintage bus. Visitors learn all about the complex processes of purification that are used to treat the 490 million litres of sewage that pass through the site each day.

So even if it's a bit of a crap day out, it's nice to know it gets done. Because while British beaches might lack the reliable sun, the balmy breezes, the beautiful women and the good food of their Italian equivalents, another thing they lack that the Mediterranean has is a plentiful supply of Richard the Thirds. And for that, we can all thank Wessex Water.

BOOZE CRUISE TO CALAIS
THE ENGLISH CHANNEL

Ah, France. Home of fine cuisine, romance, and cheap booze from hypermarkets 20 metres from the ferry terminal.

And because they have their own retail park right where you step off the boat, you don't even need to go into France. After all, nobody really likes the place. And unlike most of the country, in Calais they don't pretend they can't speak fluent English.

So you have all the best that France has to offer in one place: cheap filterless cigarettes and McDonald's selling the exotic-sounding 'Royale Cheese avec frites'. For those reasons alone, the booze cruise is a popular British day out enjoyed by all walks of British life, from Cockney alcoholics right through to heavy drinkers from Kent.

Calais was the last English-ruled town in France, primarily because the French didn't want it, and they want it even less now. Back then it was Henry V who tried to smuggle some extra duty free home in le Ford Transitte he had borrowed from his cousin. But nowadays even commoners can go shopping in Calais's off-licences.

Of course while you're there you can pick up many of the other items that France has to offer, such as illegal immigrants who will be happy to cram themselves into your wheel arch for a free trip to Dover. These are the only people in the world for whom Dover is a magical land of promise.

'Booze' – yes, most certainly there will be booze. But 'cruise'? Not so much. For most people a 'cruise' is a fortnight's sail through tropical waters sipping cocktails, not three hours spent on a floating Little Chef sipping tea made with creamer from a sachet. You are, after all, on a car ferry crossing the English Channel, one of the busiest and least picturesque stretches of water in Europe.

Defying all stereotypes, the water maintains a healthy brown complexion: a sort of mud-meets-chipboard hue that really fails to attract anyone to stare over the side of the boat. But that's all right because on the outward leg of the journey you will be stuck arguing in the 'restaurant' about the heart-stopping prices, and when you return you will be either doing the same again or rolling about legless after knocking back a box full of that stuff you found for 50p per gallon in the Little England hypermarket. And nothing sums up the golden age of travel so much as staggering across the empty deck as the rain pours down, a half-eaten Le Big Mac in one hand, half-drunk box of unidentifiable plonk in the other and your dignity in the boot of your car under 48 cans of Carrefour own-brand lager and a kilo of Golden Virginia. You can practically hear the whistle of the Orient Express.

Sadly, duty free largely disappeared under European Union law, together with freedom, curved bananas and the right to call a man in a mauve polo neck a poof. This means that every booze cruise is now accompanied by a compulsory donation to the French state, giving a bitter aftertaste to even the sweetest of tipples. They mostly spend it on retiring aged 31.

AS TO THE WAY OF LIFE OF THE ENGLISH, THEY ARE SOMEWHAT IMPOLITE, FOR THEY BELCH AT THE TABLE WITHOUT SHAME. THEY CONSUME GREAT QUANTITIES OF BEER.

Father Etienne Perlin, 1558.

BRIGHTON'S NUDIST BEACH
SUSSEX

Some days out are so dreadful that in a strange way they make you proud to be British. The nudist beach is one of them.

Swimming starkers is the right of every Briton due to the campaigning of Brighton town councillor Eileen Jakes, who in 1979 followed the barons of the Magna Carta by starting a campaign to allow the people of Brighton to get wet and salty in the buff. No doubt presuming that no one would call their bluff and choose to wear fewer clothes at the English seaside, Brighton town council signed up to her stratospherically optimistic idea and Britain's first nudey beach was born.

But quaint as it all seems now, the battle for Britain's first nudist beach was a fierce one, with Jakes facing strong opposition. In a giant boost to the Sussex tourist trade, one of her opponents, councillor John Blackman, memorably described Brighton beach in an interview as a 'flagrant exhibition of mammary glands', leading to a local surge in sales of binoculars and raincoats.

'I personally have no objection to people showing their breasts and bosoms and general genitalia to one another,' Blackman said, 'but for heaven's sake they should go somewhere more private.'

'Why should we?' they all cried, shivering as the rain poured down. 'We want to do it here! This is perfect.'

Anyway, perhaps because most people realised that they don't actually have their own beach, or perhaps because Blackman didn't know that breasts and bosoms are the same thing, Jakes won out, ensuring the right of every Briton to brave Brighton's sleet-strewn tundra even colder than they would have been in that really small 1970s swimwear.

Brighton's bold move paved the way to seaside starkersville

for Britain as a whole, and nudist beaches have since sprung up across the country in places even less hospitable to being naked than Brighton. Like Scotland.

Yes, you read right, my friend, there are nudist beaches in Scotland. On the Isle of Arran, for instance, you can throw caution to the wind and go completely naked as the Siberian gales whip around you. Lovely.

Male readers might reasonably conclude that the occasion on which they would least like to make their genitalia public is after it has been dipped in zero-degree saltwater. But like the authors of this book, they should appreciate that if they do ever decide to brave one of this country's nudist beaches, their decision to do so is no one's business but their own. After all, this is Britain, a land of liberty where every man, woman and child has the right to look like a hypothermic sex pest.

THE SOUTH EAST

LEGOLAND
WINDSOR
BERKSHIRE

There's nothing wrong with Lego. Without it we probably wouldn't have, ummm … sheds. But Lego*land*, now that's a different matter.

Rather counter-intuitively, Legoland doesn't have all that much to do with Lego. It has oodles to do with low-rent funfair rides with blocky-shaped boats which look like they have been designed on a very basic computer from the 1980s. Of course, you will have lots of time to really appreciate the design of the boats, since you will be queuing for half your life to get into one before you regret it and want to get back into the queue because it was more fun.

Lego has been branching out a lot over the past few years. Instead of teaching kids the principles of engineering by selling them kits to build houses, it now teaches kids about rock and roll excess by turning out celebrity figurines such as Amy Winehouse, Madonna and, ummm, Cliff Richard. This suits Legoland down to the ground by turning the theme park into a sort of Madame Tussauds Youth with the little fellows encouraged to denounce mummy and daddy if they don't show full commitment to The Party by taking them to the grown-up version of Madame T's output VERY SOON. Almost as if Legoland is run by the same company. Oh hang on, it is.

Interestingly, the attraction offers 'virtual queuing', which is presumably for people who really want to queue for something but can't leave the office. So instead they can do it online – a bit like people who have a virtual pet because they want a dog but don't have space for a kennel. Or people who want to have fun but without all the trouble of having it.

Legoland is right next to Windsor Castle, and the abundance

of little Lego men means the Queen believes many of her subjects are tiny and have yellow skin and funny eyes. Prince Philip thinks the Japs have invaded.

> **ALL BERKSHIRE WOMEN ARE VERY SILLY. I DON'T KNOW WHY WOMEN IN BERKSHIRE ARE MORE SILLY THAN ANYWHERE ELSE.**
>
> Mr Justice Claude Duveen, Reading County Court

WOBURN SAFARI PARK
BEDFORDSHIRE

Tigers in their natural environment of Bedfordshire. As members of the rare Home Counties species of tiger, they are obviously a little more refined than those oiks in India, and therefore prefer to avoid any of the garish publicity associated with actually being seen by the paying public.

"THE WHOLE STRENGTH OF ENGLAND LIES IN THE FACT THAT THE ENORMOUS MAJORITY OF THE ENGLISH PEOPLE ARE SNOBS.

George Bernard Shaw

"

BODYFLIGHT INDOOR SKY-DIVING
BEDFORD

The sort of suggestion that makes you wonder if the person is joking. Surely the least appropriate activity to do inside a building is skydive? Skydiving is almost certainly best performed in the sky, while things best-suited for 'indoors' include sitting about, writing reports and being annoyed by technology.

'But,' thought the inventors of Bodyflight, 'why not suck all the enjoyment out of parachuting by instead doing it in a short wind tunnel stood on its end?' That way you are rarely more than a few metres from the floor and you can avoid the unpleasant rush of adrenalin that accompanies the type of skydiving that actually involves the sky. And diving.

But it doesn't end there. After that you can try the 'Vertigo' experience, which apparently recreates the thrills of illegal, edgy and highly dangerous base jumping by safely lowering you off the roof of the building on a rope after a bit of a jump. It doesn't look an especially high, dangerously unstable or deceptively uneven building either. Perhaps they deliberately use unqualified staff to add a sense of peril, or get them noticeably drunk beforehand and try to distract them while they are working.

So instead of running the exhilarating slight risk of death or imprisonment with proper base jumping, you could perhaps get a nasty rope burn. Even at school when you climbed up the wall bars you weren't attached to a burly bloke named Ian who kept reassuring you that you were perfectly safe and couldn't fall.

And what has Bodyflight just added to its repertoire? Indoor surfing. Jesus.

WHITSTABLE OYSTER FESTIVAL
KENT

No one was more surprised by the trendy status suddenly conferred on Whitstable some time in the late 1990s than the people who actually live in this run-down fish-smelling slice of English seaside depression.

Maybe it was because Tracey Emin owned a flat in nearby Herne Bay, or perhaps the fact that Ronnie and Reggie Kray had very tenuous connections to the town, but for five years you could never open a Sunday colour supplement without casting an eye over a photograph of the same three charming fisherman's cottages that survived the perennially Tory council's mission to concrete over every square inch of land. They considered the not-concreting option, but in the end came down heavily on the side of the concreting.

Displaying the understanding of geography for which its nation is famous, the *New York Times* recently described Whitstable as 'East London's best-kept secret'. This location was even a secret from the town's residents.

But you have to hand it to the photographers – it's not easy to shoot an image that manages to exclude 98 per cent of the surroundings and fill a frame with the only buildings in a four-mile radius that aren't being urinated on by gangs of feral cider-pickled 14-year-olds. You know a town is in trouble when its charity shops are on sale.

The highlight of the Whitstable calendar is the Whitstable Oyster Festival, when once a year the foodie DFLs ('Down From London') invade the town to partake of Whitstable's only commerce other than drug trafficking, and the cabal of local tea rooms realise it is time to double their prices and watch the fat bastards roll on in to abuse the staff.

It was the Romans, apparently, who first exploited Whitstable oysters. And through thick and thin the poor bi-valves (is there another animal we would happily chew bits off while it still breathes?) have somehow attained an image of decadence. Knocking them back in the large concrete car park that is the literal and metaphorical heart of the town seems to pretty much sum up the whole Whitstable Oyster Experience – not as good as it looked in the *Times* magazine.

After the hour or so it takes to eat enough live animals to put yourself in A&E, the leisure options are limited. You could go to the block of flats that used to be a nice pub, or there's the other block that used to be the cinema. Or you could just hang about on the street looking malevolently at passers-by – an activity very popular with the townsfolk.

> **ON THE CONTINENT PEOPLE HAVE GOOD FOOD; IN ENGLAND PEOPLE HAVE GOOD TABLE MANNERS.**
>
> George Mikes, *How to be an Alien*

TEAPOT ISLAND
MAIDSTONE
KENT

People supposedly visit this odd exhibition – that isn't actually an island by any stretch of the imagination – dressed as cups. There are 6,500 teapots. It's awful if you don't like teapots. But it's probably all right if you do.

NORWICH PRIDE
NORWICH

'What be goin' ahhhn Jedro?'
  'It be them sodomites, Sam. They be restless again.'
  'Arhhhh.'

THE ENGLISH NEVER DRAW A LINE WITHOUT BLURRING IT.

Winston Churchill

THE MILL AT SONNING
DINNER THEATRE
OXFORDSHIRE

Like spray cheese in a can and Loyd Grossman, dinner theatre is a concept imported from the American colonies. The basic premise is that while you eat, some actors in the background waffle on about whatever it is they are waffling on about, and you utterly ignore them, preferring to talk to your friends.

One plus point is that there is lots of food available to hurl at the actors if the mood takes you. But the best thing about the Mill at Sonning is that you can drink during the play. If you knock back enough of the hard stuff you can forget you are in the depths of a draughty early industrial building near Reading.

> **THE ART OF COOKING AS PRACTISED BY ENGLISHMEN DOES NOT EXTEND MUCH BEYOND ROAST BEEF AND PLUM PUDDING.**
>
> Pehr Kalm, 1748

HERNE BAY PIER
SPORTS CENTRE
KENT

What is it with the people of England's coastal towns? No sooner than there's nothing good on TV, they all head down to the nearest site of historical interest to torch it.

Brighton's West Pier? Up in flames. Hastings Pier? Damp charcoal. Fleetwood Pier? Twiglets.

No one is quite sure why the pier at Weston-super-Mare went up in flames, but it was probably arson. In 2008 someone in Margate put a match to its Grade II-listed Scenic Railway, the oldest roller coaster in Britain and the last remnant of its historical Dreamland amusement park. And at Bournemouth last year, someone even managed to set the cliffs alight. The cliffs!

Still, beats watching *Match of the Day*, doesn't it?

Besides, it could have been worse. The pier at Herne Bay – only partly destroyed by fire – now features perhaps the least sensitive stroke of architectural heritage work ever completed: a corrugated iron sports centre with windows the size of stamps.

Now we don't want to be unfair. Inside, it's not a bad sports centre. There is a well-equipped gym, as well as squash and badminton courts, a creche, and even a roller-skating floor that is home to two prize-winning roller hockey teams and a roller disco. But on the outside, the place still looks like a giant Portakabin mated with a Chinese labour camp.

The Pier Sports Centre has as much connection with the sea as does a vacuum cleaner, or a pack of Chocolate Digestives. The ocean breeze is felt no more strongly there than it would be in Birmingham, or Leeds. No seagull can be heard calling, and the roller hockey teams are oblivious to giant waves, or the sound of a passing trawler's foghorn. Inside the centre, you could be anywhere. Outside, you're on an attractive seafront wondering why God has dropped a giant can of Spam on the pier.

People of Herne Bay: you may have failed to successfully burn down your pier, but we salute your originality in ruining it another way.

ALL THE FUN OF THE SEASIDE ARSON FACT-FILE:
While seaside towns including Bournemouth, Brighton, Fleetwood, Hastings and Weston-super-Mare have all burned their local attractions, Morecambe in Lancashire is the only one to have torched its attraction twice.

In 1987, some varmints started a massive fire that gutted the 'Fun City' building at the town's Frontierland Theme Park that had opened that year.

Although the building was reborn as the Crazy Horse Saloon in September the next year, a new generation of outlaws came back to finish the job in 2000, starting the rootingest, tootingest blaze in the Park's Silver Mines ride that was the final blow needed to send the already ailing Frontierland to the big saloon in the sky.

> **THE ENGLISH PUBLIC, AS A MASS, TAKES NO INTEREST IN A WORK OF ART UNTIL IT IS TOLD THAT THE WORK IN QUESTION IS IMMORAL.**
>
> Oscar Wilde

BASILDON HERITAGE TRAIL
ESSEX

The Basildon heritage trail is clearly the unfortunate result of a bitter remark by a senior member of Basildon's hard-pressed tourism department in the pub one night. The others hadn't noticed how much he had been drinking and took it as a serious suggestion.

Oddly, the Basildon heritage trail is much more literal than most, since it generally visits the sites of things which aren't there any more – old churches and other buildings which were demolished in 1948 to build the concrete behemoth that is the town of Basildon. The effect, then, of following the trail is actually to leave you feeling a bit angry about the existence of Basildon, which is surely not the intention.

Feel free to get annoyed that the Barstable Hundred Moot moots no more. At least you can pitch up at the ancient Middle Hall. Well, you can pitch up at Middle Hall Road, which is a road. Helpfully, it is connected to other roads that lead away from Basildon.

You can't fault them for trying. These days every dodgy modern town wants to tack on a bit of 'past' like a toupee; in a never-mind-the-high-suicide-rate-feel-the-history kind of way. It is rumoured that Milton Keynes is planning to rename itself as Miltonium Keynesium in one last desperate attempt to become known for something other than concrete cows and people doing their best to leave.

TOP TEN:
DAYS OUT WITH AN
OBSCURE PREMISE

1) The Bridge Across the Atlantic, Clachan Sound, Argyll

Actually it's a couple of metres wide and connects the small island of Seil with the mainland. While it is, technically, the Atlantic below you, you could jump across. When you do get to Seil, you will find a small community that specialises in killing endangered animals.

2) Talbot Hotel, Oundle, Northamptonshire

Claims to be haunted by Mary Queen of Scots. Claims.

3) Lapland Theme Parks

They're not in Lapland. If you want to go to Lapland you are free to do so, but not in Suffolk.

4) Loch Ness, The Highlands

Nessie isn't real and you can sit around all day but you will never see it.

5) Leeds Castle, West Yorkshire

In a very embarrassing blunder by Edward I, the castle was built in Leeds, Kent, meaning thousands of tourists have failed to arrive.

6) Sherlock Holmes Museum, London

It's a museum about a man that never existed, at the address where he never lived even in the books.

7) Jamaica Inn, Bodmin Moor

Known from the eponymous dull novel about violent smugglers by Daphne du Maurier. There's no smuggling any more but it is every bit as bleak as the book claims. On the other hand, the locals really do kill people for giggles.

8) Stonehenge Summer Solstice, Wiltshire

Stonehenge was constructed a couple of millennia before the Druids came along with their goats. And when the Druids did come along, even they got pissed off when the hippies started turning up.

9) Tintagel, Cornwall

Supposedly King Arthur's castle. Had he actually existed it might have been.

10)The William and Kate Tour, London

Love is a lie.

> **THE ENGLISH ARE NOT VERY SPIRITUAL PEOPLE, SO THEY INVENTED CRICKET TO GIVE THEM SOME IDEA OF ETERNITY.**
>
> George Bernard Shaw

EAST ANGLIAN RAILWAY MUSEUM
COLCHESTER
ESSEX

Colchester is Britain's oldest recorded town. The site of a Roman fortress built in AD 43, the town was once the capital of Roman Britain, and would have remained England's capital had it not been for Queen Boadicea, whose troops had a bit of a knees-up which got out of hand in AD 61. However, the Romans were just the first in a long line of groups to have left their mark on the town via its impressive historical architecture.

Like a chronological tour of the history of England, a short walk from the Saxon tower of Holy Trinity Church leads the visitor to Colchester Castle, an eleventh-century construction that boasts the largest Norman keep ever constructed, before a few minutes' stroll leads to the medieval gateway St John's Abbey, then the Tudor buildings of the 'Dutch quarters' which housed thousands of Flemish weavers when the booming wool trade made Colchester one of the richest towns in England; a further stroll leads to a host of grand Victorian buildings that bear testament to the town's stature in the industrial age too. All of which raises the question: why would you want to leave the place to go and see a museum about trains?

Don't get us wrong: steam trains are pretty cool. (Diesel trains less so, but hey-ho, they move you to places it would take ages to reach on foot.) And it's not that we have anything against the Marks Tey to Sudbury service – if you want to go from Marks Tey to Sudbury it's the perfect service. Nor that we harbour a grudge against the Reception and Railway Shop located on the ground floor of The Station Buildings built by the Great Eastern Railway in 1880, which were a replacement for the original station due to growth on the railways at the time; or to the museum's must-see database of rolling stock. It's just that, well, it's all a little outshone.

To give credit where due: if, say, we had accidentally woken up in Hull as the victim of a drunken stag-night prank and an equivalent museum were nearby, we would be all over it like a rash. But we haven't.

BEKONSCOT MODEL VILLAGE
BEACONSFIELD
BUCKINGHAMSHIRE

A little known fact about the Bekonscot Model Village is that it is a scale model of exactly what your town should look like right now. Designed and assembled by hot-shot accountant Roland Callingham in 1928, the village is the template on which every British village would have been based after Callingham and his band of upper-middle-class conspirators had overthrown Parliament and seized power.

As it happened Callingham's plan was never realised, or even formed★, but his model village still remains as a monument to what English life would have been if the country hadn't been taken over by a load of proles. Good English people go about their business, knowing their place, and no one ever claims benefits which thankfully don't exist.

Bekonscot Model Village actually comprises six little towns, of which Bekonscot is the biggest, totalling more than 200 buildings including a castle, aerodrome, harbour, manor house and farms, and even has a little coalmine where ghastly common people can be seen at work, as they should be. And since no posh town is complete without a Marks & Spencer, Bekonscot added one in 1991.

Until 1979, Bekonscot also had a model of nearby Luton Town Hall clock tower, an information board reveals, 'but fortunately this concrete monstrosity was demolished to make way for a more aesthetically pleasing building!' Whether that means in the real town or the model one is unclear, but given that almost nothing aesthetically pleasing exists in Luton, a jibe from the curators of a museum in a posh nearby village

---

★ OK, Callingham's supporters seem to be well-intentioned reformers.

is the kind of thing Luton's residents could have probably done without.

The village also contains a perfect scale model of Greenhedges, the Beaconsfield family home of Enid Blyton, author of the *Famous Five* books and one of 1930s England's leading fascists. In Blyton's *The Enchanted Village*, John and Mary visit Bekonscot. 'Oh, John – look at the little houses and churches and shops! We're much, MUCH taller than they are!' said Mary. 'They make me feel like a giant,' said John. 'Like crushing Johnny Foreigner underfoot and letting him feel the force of the British boot!'★

> **APRIL WEATHER: RAIN AND SUNSHINE BOTH TOGETHER.**
>
> English saying

★ We made that last line up.

PLUCKLEY: THE MOST HAUNTED VILLAGE IN BRITAIN
KENT

Pluckley is listed in the *Guinness World Records* as the most haunted village in Britain. Goings-on there have reduced thousands of people to tears, although this is mostly because it was also the setting for the insufferably saccharine TV series *The Darling Buds of May*. Perfick.

There are somewhere around 12 or 14 ghosts knocking about the village, depending on whom you ask and whether they are employed in the untrustworthy local tourism industry.

One of said spectres is the ghost of a highwayman, Robert Du Bois, who is speared to a tree at Fright Corner. It was a bit of a coincidence that name; a few metres on and he might have been killed at 'Unremarkable Junction', which would have been much more ironic. From there, you head up past Screaming Wood (seriously) through Ivor Bigun Drive (we made that bit up) and you come to the bridge where a ghost of a gypsy woman is said to sometimes appear as a mist. Especially around autumn. So it's a mist, in autumn, beside a large body of water. That's utterly inexplicable, isn't it? It's almost as 'Christ-I-haven't-got-a-clue-what-could-possibly-cause-that' as the fact that people have reported seeing a flickering light in the church.

In fact, it's as perplexing as the 'spectral coach', the only evidence for which is some people reporting having heard a wheeled vehicle passing along the street. That one's got us stumped too. We just can't think what could possibly account for the sound of a four-wheeled vehicle on a busy road. Not a clue. Oh, wait a second, it could be … oh, no, we were about to say 'monkeys' but that wouldn't work. So it will just have to stay a mystery unsolvable to anyone who doesn't understand what roads do.

A number of TV series have filmed in Pluckley, including *Britain's Most Haunted*. *Britain's Most Haunted* – the programme which surely wins the prize for the lowest number of exam passes among its viewers, with the sole exception of *Ultimate Force*.

Well, *Britain's Most Haunted* rocking up seems fair enough, given Pluckley's paper-thin claim to fame put about by known fable mongers. But just why did *Top Gear* do an episode from Screaming Wood? Jeremy Clarkson may have his faults, but he is not a zombie.

Many easily persuaded people have flocked to Pluckley and sworn blind that they have seen the ghosts – which is interesting because a former resident of the village named Desmond Carrington admitted decades ago to making the whole thing up for an article in *TV Times*.

> **A PERPETUAL HOLIDAY IS A GOOD WORKING DEFINITION OF HELL.**
>
> George Bernard Shaw

TOP TEN:
LEAST EDUCATIONAL
EDUCATIONAL DAYS OUT

1) The Canterbury Tales, Canterbury

The Canterbury Tales are the first masterpiece of English literature. But this exhibition with talking dummies who recite simplified versions of the stories is more like the storeroom at Madame Tussauds where they keep the off-cuts.

2) National Herb Centre, Warmington, Oxfordshire

It's a garden centre, a bit like the outdoor section at B&Q.

3) Tate St Ives, Cornwall

Nice views, pity about the pictures. Nobody likes them really.

4) Vinopolis, London

Supposedly an introduction to wine-making and connoisseur-ship. More of an introduction to their massive wine shop.

5) Mary King's Close, Edinburgh

A fascinating piece of Edinburgh's history turned into a lookalike of the Edinburgh Dungeon with more of a Plaguey theme.

6) Eden Project, Cornwall

Giant greenhouses full of plants which only make you hate environmentalists more than you already do.

7) Sutton Hoo, Woodbridge, Suffolk

All the stuff you know was found there is in the British Museum about 200 miles away.

8) Adgestone Vineyard, Isle of Wight

Perhaps the best thing that can be said of it is that it provides some relief from the Isle of Wight's strange obsession with garlic.

9) The Royal Opera House, Covent Garden, London

If you are a big fan of those Go Compare adverts on TV when some psychopath in a white tie sings the brand name over and over again until you give in and visit his sodding car insurance website, why not spend £350 on pretty much the same experience surrounded by people taking a day off from hunting?

10) Hadrian's Wall, Scotland

Look, it's a wall. There's nothing more to it. It's bricks. All it teaches you is that if you want to build a wall to keep out marauding tribes, it should probably be higher.

PICK YOUR OWN STRAWBERRIES
KENT

There are many things which have gone out of fashion over the last century. Polio and syphilis used to be all the rage but then, for some reason, they fell out of favour.

Also once popular was using your children as free labour and refusing to feed them if they asked to go to school. From the age of three or four they were quite old enough to be given such responsibilities as checking for gas down the mine or scampering up chimneys – what larks!

For those lucky enough to be born in the small segment of England which occasionally sees the sun – basically Kent – there was another treat in order: picking fruit come harvest time. Without costing the parents a penny, the little tykes could spend all day in the fields plucking hops or fruit and laughingly jumping clear of the threshing machine. Usually.

But these heady days of child exploitation are thankfully not over. It's still quite possible to benefit from underage labour in the guise of a family day out if you are mad enough to follow a sign advertising Pik Yor Own Strawbery's. On some signs, there is not a single letter that has any business being there.

For those not familiar with the experience, a day spent on a farm picking your own food is like a day spent as an illegal immigrant, except that at least illegal immigrants get paid something. Picking your own strawberries isn't paid at all – in fact, you actually pay the farmer. At least he doesn't usually confiscate your passport or try to use you as a drug mule. Well, a couple do, but they are exceptions rather than the rule.

If you were to take your car to a mechanic, attempt to fix it yourself, then bung him £400 you would come away thinking you had just shafted yourself. No such emotions with picking your own strawberries, however, when you bid a cheery farewell to the farmer who has never done an honest day's work in his life, and return to your normal house passing many shops which sell strawberries for less than you paid to pick them.

The kids think they have put one over on the farmer because they have surreptitiously eaten nearly 10p-worth of strawberries. He thinks he has put one over on you because he has.

ROYAL ASCOT
BERKSHIRE

Imagine a football match between two teams you have never heard of and, consequently, care very little about. Replace the players with animals that don't speak and all look the same, the fans with minor aristocracy, and the after-match pub trip with a tent selling plastic cups of wine for £15 a pop and – hip hip hooray! – you're all go for Royal Ascot.

Once solely a day out for members of Britain's upperish classes, horse races these days are an egalitarian experience open to anyone who wants to be patronised by a member of Britain's upperish classes.

Racehorses, which are horses ridden by men called 'jockeys', or 'dwarves', come in three distinct types: black, white and brown. Occasionally a horse can be a combination of these, rather like a cut'n'shut car from an untrustworthy local garage.

Unlike other sports, which are considered enjoyable to watch in their own right, to fully enjoy a day at Royal Ascot it is essential to bet. Otherwise a day at the races is like watching a day-long BBC1 live lottery draw when you haven't actually bought a ticket.

To place a bet you need to find a bookie. These men can still be identified by their donkey jackets and flat caps, despite the damage done to this look by David Jason in the situation comedy *Only Fools and Horses* (see UK TV Gold, Mon–Fri, Jan–Dec for details). Bookies are sometimes also known as 'turf accountants', but should not be confused with a combination of gardeners and accountants, of whom most are honest people.

A bet can be placed on different kinds of horse: a 'favourite', or an 'outsider'. Avoid any one described in the programme as a 'loser'.

A favourite is a horse that has been given low, confusing

odds by bookies such as '27–24 sideways'. A bet placed on a favourite is more likely to win than one placed on another kind of horse, but collecting your winnings may require a calculator and Stephen Hawking to act as your slowly and deliberately speaking advocate.

An outsider isn't just a horse that is outside, it is one that bookies have given more simple odds for, such as '100–1'. One of these horses will make you more money if it wins, but may also be attached to a fairground ride many miles from the track.

Another appeal of a day at Royal Ascot is the traditional hat race. The winner of the hat race is judged by the picture editor in charge of a two-page spread in the *Daily Mail* the next day, and favourites tend to be women aged below 25 with skirts well above the knee. Hat racing has come into disrepute, however, due to repeated allegations of doping.

The other main aim for a day at Ascot, is a desperate hope that the Queen will welcome you into the Royal Box. This is not as interesting as it sounds.

> **HORSE SENSE IS THE THING A HORSE HAS WHICH KEEPS IT FROM BETTING ON PEOPLE.**
>
> W C Fields

BLUEWATER SHOPPING CENTRE
GREENHITHE
KENT

At the vast, 97-acre Bluewater shopping centre 330 retailers cater for the largely imaginary needs of some 25 million shoppers a year, who are referred to not as customers but as 'guests', on the understanding that a guest is someone you invite to your home then charge them money each time they eat your food or use your stuff.

Yet the Bluewater brainwash is not always total, and at the back of their sad, tired brains, some shoppers still retain a hazy memory of a faraway youth when they had hobbies, and interests, and when life seemed to offer a richness and promise beyond the mere making and spending of money.

And, unlike the majority of shopping centres, Bluewater is not that far from a few things actually worth seeing. Outside, there are some 50 acres of landscaped garden and parkland, and seven lakes where you can enjoy the Thames Estuary's wildlife. Or you could walk to Gravesend to use the ferry over the river, which has been running since the time of the Domesday Book, and see the majestic Tilbury fort.

Or you could just wander back inside the shopping centre, where it is warm, and bright, and where you never need bother with thoughts of the past, or the future, or life, or purpose, and simply let the warm, comforting waves of cheerful commerce lap over you until Monday comes.

ROCHESTER DICKENS WEEK
KENT

An inexplicably growing phenomenon in commuter towns nationwide, the Victorian Evening is an idea dreamed up by local councils to bring some Dickensian magic to high street shops in the run-up to Christmas. And having been mentioned in a book by Dickens, Rochester isn't backward about coming forward on this score.

The concept is a simple one, and involves inviting the otherwise-normally-dressed public to dress up in frock coats, top hats or big dresses to eat roast chestnuts, drink mulled wine and spend money in local shops rather than Tesco, which is rumoured to need very little public support.

Of course, if it were a real Dickens evening, the adults in the family would all die of some terrible and painful infection, leaving the young children to walk barefoot to their mysterious and loopy aunt's house in another part of the country, only to discover she died two days before and left everything to the cat. Not to mention the brutal murder of some prostitutes. Christmas magic.

Instead, there is also normally some painful 'entertainment' in the form of a performance by warbling local schoolchildren who want to be at home where it's warm, late night shopping for people who like to shop late and at night, and the mayor might make an appearance to turn on the genuine Dickensian Christmas lights in his Mr T chains.

Dickens evenings – or 'evenings' as Dickens would have described them – also help people feel festive for Christmas because the days that people think of affectionately are those at the end of *A Christmas Carol*. The characters of the book are remembered for their (eventual) heart-warming honesty, goodwill and general Christmas cheeriness. In reality, of course, the rest of the year for the Cratchit family would have been spent in ceaseless work of soul-destroying tedium – the likes of which make working in a British Gas call centre seem like the job of chief masseur at the Playboy Mansion.

So unless your child is in the school choir, you particularly love school choirs or you are the mayor of your town, there is nothing much to do except look at other people dressed funny, eat burnt conkers and try to enjoy mincemeat-flavoured wine while you get colder and colder. As the council really knew all along, this will soon mean you take shelter in one of the shops and end up buying something that you really don't want, like a new toaster you don't need. What a glorious evening: being tricked into buying electrical goods while wearing a top hat.

THE
MIDLANDS

MONSTER TRUCK NATIONALS
SANTA POD RACEWAY
NORTHAMPTONSHIRE

Admit it, you like monster trucks. Don't be shy – we all do. Especially when they burst out onto the track, running over a few ordinary cars. The only problem here is that it gets an eensy-weensy bit samey after a while.

When you come along the Monster Truck Nationals ('It's Judgement Day'*) you get to see a whole lot of guest Monster Trucks, but the crowd's favourite is Podzilla. I don't know if you can see what they have done there, but just to explain: the name is a 'portmanteau' word combining 'Pod' and the second two syllables of 'Godzilla', the patron saint of angry Japanese lizards.

Then they're off! Driving up and down the track and over and around obstacles like a form of Crufts performed by huge evil robots. Sometimes over other puny cars probably driven by people who have never even SEEN a monster truck before. And if that weren't enough, there is also Extreme Wrestling on offer. Wrestling a monster truck? Well, no – that would be Beyond Extreme Wrestling. And it's Extreme enough as it is.

Where do you even buy Monster Trucks? We have looked and we have looked, but just haven't found one on the open market. We would buy one, we just don't know what they run on. We thought it was monsters, but apparently that's wrong.

---

* And why do judges never say that through a microphone when they are about to pass sentence? It would scare the crap out of most criminals.

ALTHORP HOUSE
ALTHORP
NORTHAMPTON

Once just one stately home among many, Althorp House in Northamptonshire received a major shot in the arm in 1997 with the death of its most famous former inhabitant, Diana, Princess of Wales and Hearts.

The ancestral home of the Spencer family is now a place of pilgrimage for *Daily Express* readers, and is rivalled only by the Diana Memorial Fountain in London's Hyde Park for the number of Grief Vampires that gather to feast on the blood of someone else's tragedy each year.

Saint Diana is buried on an island in a lake that would once have been described as 'peaceful' before half the readership of *OK!* magazine began turning up on a daily basis to swap tales of how the royal family had had to issue restraining orders to keep them away and how often they send Prince Charles their own turds in the post.

> **HOLIDAYS HAVE NO PITY**
>
> Eugenio Montale

WALSALL ILLUMINATIONS
WEST MIDLANDS

Like the Blackpool Illuminations, only without the jet-set glamour.

> IT IS POSSIBLE THAT THERE ARE UGLIER TOWNS IN THE WORLD, BUT IF SO I DO NOT KNOW ABOUT THEM AND I CONSIDER MYSELF BETTER THAN AVERAGELY TRAVELLED.
>
> Theodore Dalrymple on Walsall

CADBURY WORLD
BIRMINGHAM

If you own a factory that makes chocolate, offering a good time to the 99 per cent of the public that enjoy eating chocolate should be something of a no-brainer. Tell that to Cadbury UK plc, however, who have somehow avoided it despite the most promising of starts.

The problem with Cadbury World in a (Fruit &) nutshell is this: due to restrictive health and safety laws for which we can probably blame the EU without any evidence, Cadbury World is the chocolate factory visit that doesn't include a visit to the chocolate factory.

It's not especially hard to guess why kids or the morbidly obese would want to visit Cadbury World. It does seem to hold out promise of being stuffed with so much chocolate that people you pass on the street will develop type 2 diabetes. It is a little bit annoying, then, that you hardly get within spitting distance of a Curly Wurly.

Instead of seeing Flakes trundle past on production lines, you are treated to a series of video presentations/propaganda on how great Cadbury's chocolate is. You also get thrown a few chocolate buttons like a Victorian beggar with your nose pressed to the glass of a pudding shop.

And so it continues, until in a splendid stroke of unintentional irony, the 'Making Chocolate' zone actually offers the chance to watch a series of interactive videos about how chocolate is made – the chocolate factory equivalent of, say, visiting Hampton Court Palace to sit in room looking at recent photographs of Hampton Court Palace.

The exhibition of packaging is the nearest one gets to actually seeing chocolate being produced – the wrapper, of course, being what every child finds most exciting about a chocolate bar. And just in case any child might have accidentally retained a single brown crumb of enthusiasm at this point, Cadbury World's promotional literature cautions that 'we can't guarantee that the machine will be running'.

Don't worry – you can come away with as much chocolate as you want. You just have to buy it in the handy shop. And there are some special items they have on sale there that you can't buy anywhere else in the world – that's because they are the misshapen or B-grade produce. Think how popular you will be at school when you offer around your straight Curly Wurlys. Or your completely solid Flake.

Hopefully now that Cadbury is owned by Kraft, we can look forward to children being treated to small pouches of Kraft cheesy pasta with every visit. They won't know how to thank you enough. Willy Wonka sleeps soundly tonight.

> **THE LONGEST CHAPTER IN DEUTERONOMY HAS NOT CURSES ENOUGH FOR AN ANTI-BROMINGHAM.**
>
> John Dryden on Birmingham

DUDLEY CASTLE
WEST MIDLANDS

Christ knows what there is worth defending in Dudley. Seriously, there's nothing.

66

THE ENGLISH THINK THAT INCOMPETENCE IS THE SAME THING AS SINCERITY.

Quentin Crisp

99

THE LADY GODIVA CLOCK
COVENTRY

There's an assumption that any town with a cathedral must be quite nice. Coventry very much kills this theory and then dances a merry jig on its grave.

During the Second World War German bombers happily flocked to Coventry in order to break the residents' spirit, and the peacetime rebuilding of the town centre pretty much finished the job they started. At least the Germans tried to make up for it with Kraftwerk.

Now any tourist who thought he was going somewhere else will sooner or later stumble across the town's premier clock-and-sexual-predator-based attraction: The Lady Godiva Clock.

Gaze up from the chic town centre Lady Godiva news kiosk and you see the outline of a large clock in the wall. At least you see the most basic parts of clockery: hands and hour markers, but no actual clock face, which might have ruined the enjoyable 'bricky' effect. As the hour comes around, and the residents of Coventry are very aware of each hour ticking past, so does Coventry's most famous exhibitionist daughter, Lady Godiva.

You remember the story from school: Lady G was an Anglo-Saxon noblewoman who rode naked through Coventry in some truly unfathomable protest against taxation. Her husband, a little surprised by this, ordered the local people not to look. Only local sex maniac Peeping Tom was sensible enough to cop a quick eyeful – a clever move because *Razzle* would not be invented for 900 years. No doubt Lady G had a strong economic argument based on fiscal policy, but really all people remember are her knockers.

So a mechanical Lady G now pops out of a window below the clock in her birthday suit, with her bits covered by long hair (this is, after all, a family show). It's the nude-fiscal-policy-criticising memorial she would have wanted.

Then, hot on her saucy heels, comes Peeping Tom. In contrast to normal sexual deviant behaviour, however, he isn't touching himself inappropriately or wearing Crocs. This is therefore the only known example of a man disappointing families by not indulging in public masturbation. Of course some parents act in a hypocritical fashion by encouraging their kids to enjoy the spectacle, while simultaneously telling them to stay well away from similar sights in the local parks or on webcams. To be fair to the gentlemen who spend much of their time in Coventry's parks giving themselves treats, it is probably the most interesting thing to do in Coventry.

The deviancy-themed fun doesn't stop with the clock, however. Just around the corner people out shopping are eagerly watched over by a statue of Peeping Tom. No doubt Coventry should probably be congratulated for its bold step in making a sex pest its town symbol.

> **I'VE ALWAYS FELT ENGLAND WAS A GREAT PLACE FOR A COMIC TO WORK. IT'S AN ISLAND AND THE AUDIENCE CAN'T RUN VERY FAR.**
>
> Bob Hope

THE WATTELISK
BIRMINGHAM

Surely one of the oddest ways imaginable to commemorate a nineteenth-century engineer who helped drive the industrial revolution is to produce a statue of him in the form of a totem pole carved out of a large stone obelisk. But that didn't stop the visionary sculptor behind this piece of extraordinary silliness really going for broke.

Your bog-standard sculptor may have gone for a vaguely faithful visual representation of James Watt, perhaps standing beside one of his inventions, most of which centred around steam-powered industrial production. The flyer-and-bobbin cotton spinning technique, for instance, was one of Watt's lasting gifts to mankind and was therefore completely ignored by the sculptor.

Because the Wattelisk's creator went a bit 'lateral' in his thinking, instead plumping for a four-lump obelisk, which, for most people, is instantly suggestive of a towering bonfire of public cash.

The bottom lump is your average shapeless rock, on top of that is something a bit headish, then comes something a bit facey, and finally – oh look! – it's James Watt. It might be just what he would have wanted; but then again it might not. It's almost certainly not what he would have expected.

Rumours are circulating that Birmingham council plans to produce a memorial to Richard Arkwright, creator of the Water Frame cotton process, in the form of a gun-toting Japanese manga character atop a beetle rearing on its hind legs.

SHAKESPEARE'S BIRTHPLACE
STRATFORD-UPON-AVON
WARWICKSHIRE

Slightly less pleasant than a visit to Shakespeare's birth canal, this is indeed a trip to the place where he spent his early years, but apart from the four walls there's pretty much bugger all that is original. There are video presentations aplenty, yet genuine Bardic memorabilia is largely non-existent, most of the stuff in the house simply being items a bit reminiscent of the era. So it's 'The Shakespeare family may have had curtains like these. Then again they might not. We haven't got a clue to tell you the truth, we bought these at Asda.'

And when you get right down to it, even the structure of the house has been remodelled since little Will was knee-high to a grasshopper. So you're visiting a house which is different, and looking at items which are entirely unrelated.

Stratford-upon-Avon is undeniably a pretty little town, although you will be so sick of overpriced cream teas by the time you leave that you risk having a violent Pavlovian reaction to scones for the rest of your days. They are so ubiquitous they should probably get their own representation on the council.

Elsewhere in the town you can go one better than visiting Shakespeare's birthplace – you can visit his deathplace. New Place, where he spent his final years before dying of a cold, also goes one better than the original family home by going to all the effort of having been knocked down 200 years ago by a vicar with violent tendencies. You actually visit the house next door, which seems to be really testing what you will put up with. If you paid to go to Windsor Palace but were directed instead to a two-bedroom flat down the road where you could look through someone's postcards of Windsor, you might just feel cheated. Same applies, Stratford.

CITY OF CAVES
NOTTINGHAM

An afternoon knocking about in the sewers below Nottingham is a hard sell for anyone, and hats off to the City of Caves marketing department for doing their best with this one.

The caves – some natural, some man-made, all damp – might appeal to some people who like the idea of escaping from society/justice but it's difficult to see why the people of modern Nottingham would want to ape their forlorn ancestors who often hung about down here for a laugh.

'Make all your wishes come true!' their marketing material says, although not specifying that this only works if all your wishes include walking around in some potholes below the city's main shopping centre and really hoping that you don't get lost.

'Meet real cave dwellers!' it continues. Thanks, but we would rather not. You are told that the 'cave dwellers' are seeking refuge from the world above, so you're disturbing criminals in a dark sewer. There's no way anything could go wrong there.

And for kids who thought they were going on an Indiana Jones adventure, only to discover it's more of an underground car park adventure with the potential for coming out smelling of drains, there might be a tinge of resentment.

As well as the chance to breathe bad air and smell of drains, the caves also offer the chance to join one of the regular 'paranormal happenings' held there. One can only imagine the fun to be had at one o'clock in the morning when you are alone underground, out of contact with society and the police, with a man dressed as a medieval sorcerer who believes he hears the voices of long-dead murderers. And they're not asking him the football scores.

'What's that Hatchet Bob? What did you say? By why would

I? He's no danger to us. Oh, is that true? He's one of them, you say. Well, perhaps it is for the best. Yes, like you say, utterly silent down here. Silent as … what was that you said? "The grave." Yes, I suppose you're right. No one will ever know a thing …'

> ## TO DISAGREE WITH THREE-FOURTHS OF THE BRITISH PUBLIC ON ALL POINTS IS ONE OF THE FIRST ELEMENTS OF SANITY, ONE OF THE DEEPEST CONSOLATIONS IN ALL MOMENTS OF SPIRITUAL DOUBT.
>
> Oscar Wilde

COALPORT CHINA MUSEUM
SHROPSHIRE

'The National Collections of Caughley and Coalport china in the magnificent old Coalport China works. Rich colours, bright glazes and exquisite decoration.' It's hard to resist the urge to smuggle in a bull and make it angry.

> **MY FATHER WAS IN THE CIVIL SERVICE. I CAN REMEMBER STANDING IN A BUS SHELTER IN THE POURING RAIN, AND THAT WE WERE ALLOWED CANDY FLOSS AT THE END OF THE HOLIDAY IF WE HAD BEHAVED.**
>
> Honor Blackman

THE LOST CITY OF LICHLANTIS
UM...

Last year Lichfield was named in a list of cities that are disliked by British travellers – slightly unfairly, at it transpired, given that more than half of those polled admitted that they didn't even know where it was.

The city finished tenth in the list of 'No Entry Cities' in a survey of 5,000 people conducted by luxury hotels group Travelodge, with Bradford – the Paris of the West Yorkshire Conurbation – topping the list.

Many of the cities were singled out for being ugly, boring or extremely dangerous, but poor Lichfield's appearance on the list came after 59 per cent of those asked simply had no idea where it was.

The survey went on to claim that the places on the list were at risk of becoming 'lost cities' to future generations as a result of poor geographic knowledge, raising the amusing prospect of Wakefield or Bradford disappearing into legend like Atlantis.

Visit Britain communication director Patricia Yates said: 'If we do not invest in discovering the cities that make Great Britain great, these cities will be lost to future generations.'

Unless they buy a satnav.

THE ENGLISH ARE ALWAYS READY TO ADMIRE ANYTHING SO LONG AS THEY CAN QUEUE UP.

George Mikes, *How to be an Alien*

THE NORTH

THE GREAT NORTH RUN – IN FANCY DRESS
NEWCASTLE TO SOUTH SHIELDS

According to a recent article in the *Observer*, we're all wearing fancy dress these days. All of us. All the time. There is hardly a day that goes by when we're not in fancy dress. But despite the claim appearing in the *Observer*, it is partly true.

From all the blokes on stag weekends dressed as chickens or their favourite twentieth-century dictators ('Mussolini! Brilliant! What will you do next, you nutter? What's that? Organise a Fascist coup? OK, that's going a bit too far. No, I don't think it's "cheeky".') to mad-for-it clubbers dressed as their favourite muppet there do seem to be more people wearing clothing inappropriate to the environment than twenty years ago when most people dressed non-fancy. And there is no greater concentration of the other-than-sensibly-attired than towards the rear of the Great North Run waving at uncomfortable strangers.

On the face of it, running a marathon sharing a wool pantomime horse costume would seem a particularly foolish idea. There's just no way it will help your finishing time. And the whole 'but it's for charity' plea just doesn't wash. After all, if Roger from sales asks you to sponsor him to run a half marathon to raise money for Cancer Research, it would be conspicuously mean if you refused him solely on the basis that he is not dressed as an orc. You might even go so far as to say that no one would. The only conclusion? Roger just wants to dress as an orc. He probably has done so for some time.

Yes, it might get you noticed – in the way crashing a car into seven people waiting at a bus stop will get you noticed – but at the end of the day, the people who come up to you and start talking because of your costume will always remember you as 'that guy who was dressed as a Dalek'. Not your name. You might end up on the news if you keel over and die, like a number of idiots dressed as chickens each year. But you will still only be 'That bloke who died dressed like a chicken.'

DRACULA EXPERIENCE
WHITBY

Legend has it that Bram Stoker had the idea for the novel *Dracula* after a nightmare induced by a dodgy crab consumed in Whitby. It's perhaps the only case of a major work of literature inspired by an evening of vomiting, and Whitby is understandably proud.

Anyway, the novel sets the seaside town as the scene of Nosferatu's arrival in Britain in a coffin, and Whitby remains a popular destination with Romanian package holiday tourists to this day.

This vampire link has been grabbed with two pale hands by the town's tourist industry, which has been a bit stuck since people in the local area discovered there really is more to life than Whitby. There is, for instance, Grimsby. This means that Whitby now hosts an annual Goth festival for those who aren't understood by their parents/society/anyone else but have no trouble at all deciding what colour clothes to wear when they get up in the morning. Also making the town slightly unhappier than it would have been is The Dracula Experience – an attraction that attempts to instil fear of the undead using a combination of ZX Spectrum computer technology and the local unemployed dressed in their grandparents' clothes.

'As you enter a dreadful fear will come upon you,' The Dracula Experience claims. 'The Count's mysterious appearance and frightening warning will make you wonder if you should have come to Whitby ...' A description honest to a fault.

So you stumble through, occasionally stopping to make a phone call or read a newspaper you have brought with you, through various depictions of scenes from Stoker's novel you half remember through the mist of Whitby rain. Highlights include a room containing a dummy in a sailor's costume tied to a mock ship's wheel with string. The dummy looks even more embarrassed than you are to be there.

The high point of the experience is near the end when a vampress puppet 'flies' along a wire towards you. It's not Chucky, the demon doll; it's not even his mum. It's more like Finger Mouse after you have taunted him with a bit of cheese. Being alone heightens any sense of fear, and there is a very good chance you will be alone while you walk through the mercifully few rooms. That's because most people know it is rubbish.

The Dracula Experience is supposed to leave you a gibbering wreck, fearing nightfall. It really just leaves you fearing you have wasted £7.50 and half an hour of your life. Perhaps it is why Goths always look so down in the dumps.

> " THE BRITISH DO NOT EXPECT HAPPINESS. I HAD THE IMPRESSION, ALL THE TIME THAT I LIVED THERE, THAT THEY DO NOT WANT TO BE HAPPY; THEY WANT TO BE RIGHT. Quentin Crisp "

SURFING IN HARTLEPOOL
CLEVELAND

Recreating the 1950s Californian surfing experience a stone's throw from Denmark was always going to be a stretch. Swapping Ford Thunderbirds with their tops down, and beautiful blonde girls with their tops off, for uninsured Ford Transits and single mothers on benefits is not a like-for-like swap.

That doesn't stop many wishful thinkers from slamming on the Beach Boys, strapping their boards to the top of their parents' four-door saloon cars and heading for the waves to risk life and limb in the hypothermic conditions.

Just so we're clear, the authentic sound of Hartlepool isn't the Beach Boys, it's Les Dawson. Less 'California Girls', more 'Knees Up Mother Brown'.

Hartlepool's surfers probably also use fake words like 'gnarly' and 'bodacious' because they were in that film they saw. The hand gestures are beyond them, though, because their fingers have seized up and turned yellow.

Helpfully, the council has provided a lifeguard station so you can stand and watch as the surfers 'shoot the wave' and 'get into difficulty' before 'drowning'.

On days when the surfers go out – 'Idiot Days' as they are known locally – you can see the *Hartlepool Times*'s photographer on the seafront taking snaps to use as the 'before tragedy struck' image on the front cover. And beside him, the local undertaker warming up his tape measure.

YORKSHIRE SCULPTURE PARK
WAKEFIELD

The people behind London's Tate Modern gallery pulled off an amazing coup when they launched it in 2000: obtaining an unwanted old building, filling it mostly full of the least-celebrated works by unknown artists and turning it into a booming tourist attraction overnight. People flocked there to see things they despised and resented for being purchased with public money.

But the coup wasn't an original one, nor was it executed with as much panache as when the trick was first pulled off, by the Yorkshire Sculpture Park. Not only did the Yorkshire Sculpture Park do it twenty years earlier, but as the name suggests, it also didn't even bother to obtain a building.

The park was the UK's first sculpture park, and describes itself as a 'gallery without walls' – the art gallery equivalent of how a homeless person might have a home, or the emperor might have new clothes.

Artists working at YSP including American sculptor James Turrell, who turned a deer shelter into a sculpture, even though most people – and deers – would actually have preferred the precise opposite. Also knocking about the place was Britain's Andy Goldsworthy, whose three-month exhibition there was named 'Parkland', both artists taking their inspiration from the park's natural environment and the chance to do that sort of thing for a living instead of having to go into an office every day or make proper things like boxes. The word 'parkland', of course, shares a suspiciously large number of letters with the word 'park', which suggests Goldsworthy didn't put much effort into thinking up a name.

Many of the sculptures are quite good, and if you are lucky enough to visit on the north of England's annual sunny day, it's not that bad a day out. Since the 1990s, however, the park has faced up to the fact that it is based near Leeds, not near Lisbon or Los Angeles, and started using indoor exhibition spaces and a temporary tent-like structure called the Pavilion Gallery, which might not have central heating but is better than being outside in the rain.

Luckily, the lack of walls to encase the artworks has not extended to the shop which boasts at least four of them that work just fine against the weather conditions. So there is no need to worry that any of the staff will get cold and wet – it will only be the public at risk.

In the unlikely event that the authors of this book are invited to contribute a sculpture to the park, we already have an idea in mind. Like Turrell, Goldsworthy and many other artists who have displayed work there, our sculpture will take its inspiration from the surrounding environment. Cast in brass, it will take the form of a forlorn monkey-like figure neutered by the cold, and huddled against the natural environment of Yorkshire.

> **IF ALL THE YEAR WERE PLAYING HOLIDAYS, TO SPORT WOULD BE AS TEDIOUS AS TO WORK.**
>
> William Shakespeare, *Henry IV, Part I*

BYLAND ABBEY – 'THE SECOND-LARGEST COLLECTION OF FLOOR TILES IN EUROPE'
RYDALE
YORKSHIRE

'The second-largest collection of floor tiles in Europe'. That's some pretty tough talking. Let's be clear here: Byland Abbey is not claiming to be 'in the top five European abbeys with regards to number of floor tiles', it is putting its marker down on the number 2 spot. In abbey terms, that is like kicking open the swinging doors of a Wild West saloon bar and calling all the other abbeys sissies.

Byland, like many medieval abbeys, is looking a bit the worse for wear. The fact that it was pretty much smashed to the ground during the Dissolution of the sixteenth century probably has a good deal to do with it. But it does have some stories. Perhaps the best is that of Wimund, one of its twelfth-century bishops.

A bit of a jack-of-all-trades, Wimund was not at all content with being a twelfth-century bishop. So, contrary to normal church practice, he became a pirate too. Juggling his episcopal duties with seaborne rape-and-pillage attacks and slaughtering his way through southern Scotland must have been a nightmare in scheduling terms, but he did it pretty well for years, until his enemies had him sneakily blinded and castrated. During his period of dual employment, we wonder what his birthday parties must have been like. Presumably they were pretty divided affairs.

His end was certainly a bitter blow for students of English bishopry/piracy. But perhaps it was just as well to go out on a high note – after all, once you have been a bishop/pirate, where do you go from there? Rabbi/ninja? Buddhist monk/zombie shape-shifter? Like that difficult third album, it's always going to be a disappointment to your early fans.

THE MUSEUM OF LAKELAND LIFE
KENDAL
CUMBRIA

The Museum of Lakeland Life documents the fascinating history of the Lake District and its inhabitants, as well as all of the moderately interesting history of the Lake District and its inhabitants, plus all the other history of the Lake District and its inhabitants.

But then people don't visit the Lake District for its museums, they go for the great outdoors. The Museum of Lakeland Life might just as well have been called 'The Museum of Lakeland Life – Something to Do If It's Raining'. They probably found the name was too long for the gift shop pencils. The museum contains a series of tableaux vivants – which is French for 'models' – that narrate the stories of the now lost Lakeland trades and professions that, as it happens, weren't a million miles away from the now-lost professions everywhere else.

Still, the weather doesn't look like it's going to clear up, so you might as well crack on. And if there's anything apart from the beautiful scenery to celebrate about the Lake District, by God will this museum celebrate it. Like folk history? Enjoy looking at the assorted possessions of Lake District author Arthur Ransome? Then you'll love the museum's exhibitions on those plus its in-depth history of the Arts & Crafts design movement - all under one rainproof roof.

Still raining and the kids are beginning to play up? Well then why not cross the town and visit the Quaker Tapestry Museum, a celebration of centuries of Quaker thought and understanding exhibited in the immortal medium of tapestry.

No, you're right, I suppose it's not raining all that hard. All right, we'll go back to the hotel.

YORK DUNGEON
YORKSHIRE

If you listen carefully outside the York Dungeon, you can hear the bottom of the barrel being scraped. Where do you go if you can't get a job as a rabies victim at the London Dungeon? Why not try York? So it's a bit like buying from the reduced counter at some dodgy supermarket – you really didn't think it would ever come to this but there you are working out if a yoghurt three days out of date will do you 'that much' harm.

The York Dungeon boasts that it hosts ten different shows, performed by seven actors. Which – forgive us if our maths is a little rusty – means that either the actors swap costumes in between shows, or a minimum of three of the shows are performed by robots or by helpful local elves who scamper in during the dead of afternoon and put on a wee play for the amusement of the humans. They must be local elves, because the price of hotel accommodation in York is extortionate.

Interestingly, during the Dungeon's 'Ghosts of York' show, you are promised that you will be enveloped by 'a feeling of resentment and anger', which considering you have paid £15 to get in is surprisingly mild. Even the Dalai Lama would be feeling a certain amount of 'resentment and anger'.

Another attraction is 'Bloody Vikings' which, depending on how it is read, sounds a bit underwhelming as in: 'Bloody Vikings, they never clean up after themselves. It's always Muggins here who has to put away their big helmets and remember to turn off the TV.' Or 'I was going to go to Halfords today for some new spark plugs but it's a bank holiday so it will be full of bloody Vikings.'

MUSEUM OF THE HISTORY OF EDUCATION
LEEDS

SCOTLAND STREET SCHOOL MUSEUM
GLASGOW

Taking kids to a museum about education really is adding insult to injury. Education about education is actually quantum boredom. It is tedium squared – quadratic ennui. Yet, like Mafia godfathers hell-bent on harassing children, these two museums have carved up the nation into 'manors' to give countrywide coverage of a subject that children do their best to forget whenever they are not in the classroom.

The Museum of the History of Education even has a boring name. It contains 'extensive archive material including teacher training records, pupil and teacher work, and administrative records such as school log books'. And what child wouldn't leap at the chance to read old administrative records and school log books? From there he or she could go on to reading historical records of production in minor industries, or lists of other people they had never heard of.

The Scotland Street School Museum gets around the knotty problem of kids brightening up whenever they are outside school by actually recreating a Victorian school, so that any pupils brought here will instantly understand they are not on an enjoyable field trip. Presumably the management tones down the historically accurate chance of 12-year-olds being beaten unconscious by teachers with heavy sticks or falling pregnant at 14 before a life of ceaseless toil ended only by the welcoming soil. But to remove it entirely would spoil the atmosphere.

THE QUILT MUSEUM
YORK

The museum is proud to be the only one in Europe dedicated to quilts, not having stopped for a moment to wonder why that is.

Allow us to explain. It is largely because quilts are very useful items if you want to be warm in bed. Perhaps you wouldn't mind seeing the odd one or two in a museum if they are of quite exceptional historical note, such as one a pope died under or one sewn by Jimmy Nail during breaks in his prestigious 1990s music career. But an entire building bursting at the seams with the things is just going too far. It is, you might say, 'blanket coverage'.

But don't worry if you can't get to the Quilt Museum, which is run by the Quilters' Guild. (We can't wait to go to one of their Christmas parties. We bet they're a riot – not to mention very cosy.) Because you can download an informative podcast on the history of quilts from the International Quilts Study Centre – the NASA of the quilts world.

The museum has an education programme so that teachers can have a day off from their proper job of smoking nervously in the staff room, and drag the kids along to learn about the history of bedspreads. It is, at least, a really good place to take a nap.

Don't ask the Quilt Museum about duvets; they wouldn't even spit on them.

THE ANGEL OF THE NORTH
GATESHEAD

THE B OF THE BANG
MANCHESTER

A truly impressive statue to man's hopes and dreams for the future, The Angel of the North regularly distracts motorists on the A1 from Gateshead to Newcastle. It might not be to everyone's taste, but it beats Manchester's attempt to emulate its success – the oddly named sculpture The B of the Bang – by just staying up.

The B of the Bang was unexpectedly commissioned to mark the 2002 Commonwealth Games in Manchester. Its name was inspired by a comment from athlete Linford Christie, who once said that he started running on 'the b of the bang'. As such, it is the only major work of art inspired by Christie's linguistic philosophy. This was perhaps its first mistake.

The second mistake was constructing and erecting the bloody thing. An 18-month delay gave the sculpture – designed to look like an exploding firework but actually looked like a toilet brush – the nickname 'The G of the Bang'.

The next problem was that six days before the official unveiling by Christie, a bit fell off and, like a scene from *Flash Gordon*, a massive metal spear went hurtling to the ground. This incident gave the structure its second nickname: KerPlunk, after the game popular among 1970s kids who didn't know anything better than to pull straws out of a metal tube in the hope that a marble wouldn't fall down. They were simpler times, less enjoyable times.

By this point, the structure had cost £1.42m – more than twice the original quote. In 2009, after a little legal action, the council eventually ordered that it be taken apart and put into 'storage' as the 'only practical alternative'. Presumably the word 'alternative' was used in the sense of 'we have two alternatives: pull the bloody thing down, or just let it fall on people walking past – which do you prefer?'

PREMIER INN HONEYMOON SPECIAL
HULL

What young girl doesn't dream of hearing these special words from her beloved: 'Marry me, darling, and we will have the honeymoon at the Premier Inn (Hull City Centre branch). This is but a token of how much I love you. For two full nights we will make perfect love exploring each other's minds and bodies; but mostly bodies. Also, there will be crisps.'

Hull is known as the city of lovers. Don Juan lived there as a young man, learning from Casanova and John Prescott.

And what cries love more clearly than a £58 honeymoon special including Premier Inn's all-you-can-eat breakfast buffet. Nothing is more romantic than fried bread. But those lovers among the Premier Inn management know their game. They are aware that after all the perfectly sexual love, newlyweds can often get cold, having forgotten to pack suitable night clothing.

This is where they step in.

For they chuck in a nightie and stripey pyjamas. Both are from the designers of Primark.

Classy. And sexy. At once. Claxy.

> **THERE IS A FEELING WHICH PERSISTS IN ENGLAND THAT MAKING A SANDWICH INTERESTING, ATTRACTIVE, OR IN ANY WAY PLEASANT TO EAT IS SOMETHING SINFUL THAT ONLY FOREIGNERS DO.**
>
> Douglas Adams, *So Long, and Thanks for All the Fish*

THE ARNDALE CENTRE
MANCHESTER

Manchester's Arndale Centre is the Bluewater of the North, only with more glue sniffing and a higher shell-suit count. Thankfully, the Arndale Centre is nowhere near any of that nasty countryside and its builders managed to clear away a lot of horrid eighteenth-century buildings to give it a modern, concrete home. At least at Bluewater the security guards bother to stop the shoplifters; at the Arndale Centre the teenage scallies wouldn't get away with more than £6 of stock in one carload so it's hardly worth the effort.

But you can't really blame the local 14-year-olds for hanging out at the mall – after all, they don't have anywhere else to go during the school day – and it teaches them just as much as more 'formal' education. They learn maths skills when working out whether they will earn more from selling five necklaces from Claire's Accessories hidden in their bras, or two iPods twocked from Currys and stuffed down their pants. They learn about foreign culture from Pizza Hut; and driving skills from performing high-speed handbrake turns in the car park.

Really, the Arndale Centre is a microcosm of the world. You can see the whole cycle of life as teenage girls get knocked up in the toilets and old people give up the ghost waiting in line in Aldi. Even Spud-U-Like would have been a more dignified way to go.

YORVIK BRASS RUBBING CENTRE
YORK

Do you remember how much fun brass rubbing was when you were at school? That's right: none at all. But don't rely solely on prejudice – go into the Yorvik Brass Rubbing Centre with an open mind, and then you can have all your prejudices confirmed by evidence.

At the Yorvik Brass Rubbing Centre you won't be presented with the dull old brasses to rub; instead you will be presented with dull fake new brasses to rub. Replicas of old brasses are a-plenty at this attraction, which markets itself as 'the ideal quieter activity for daytime or evenings'. They're certainly bang-on when they describe brass rubbing as a bit on the quiet side. You could have four hundred brass rubbers standing shoulder to shoulder in a room and you could hear insects walking. It would make for the world's most relaxing team sport and could be topped off with a spot of wood-feeling or view-looking.

Quite why you might want to make a rough tracing of a door knob is anyone's guess. But you are, the centre makes clear, allowed to keep your rubbings. So you needn't worry about copyright issues regarding showing your work.

It's funny how much 'brass rubbing' sounds like a double entendre, but isn't. It's a single entendre looking for another one. So much so, in fact, that 'brass rubbing' sounds like the sort of thing you shouldn't be taking children to. It *is* the sort of thing you shouldn't be taking children to, but only because they will be bored.

SINGLES NIGHT AT ASDA
PRINCESS WAY
BURNLEY

You can see the logic: single people need to meet other singles; single people also need to buy Domestos. Some single people also need razor blades and a huge bottle of aspirin representing 'a way out', but the Burnley (Princess Way) branch of Asda hopes to pre-empt that stage.

And nothing says classy and exotic lover like shopping at Asda. Johnny Depp is known to nip in for a few sausages, milk and some red hot lovin' on his way home. He also likes their recent addition of financial services packages. After all, everybody needs a sensible life insurance plan.

Meeting a potential soulmate while out buying ham or an all-day-breakfast in a can therefore offers the ideal lifestyle solution for today's cash-rich, time-poor singleton.

So much so, in fact, that there are socially recognised signs to indicate your availability. A single passion fruit on top of your shopping apparently means you are unattached. Passion, you see. Or, of course, it could mean you like passion fruit but you don't eat more than one at once and it was the most recent item you put in your trolley. A pack of dates might suggest that you are looking for a date – but it could mean that you are looking for ten sticky dates in a row before deciding not to try one again till next Christmas.

For men, a single marrow on top of your shopping means you are boasting.

In order to avoid hilarious singles-night misunderstandings just like out of an early episode of *Friends*, Asda (Princess Way, Burnley branch) helpfully hands out ribbons to shoppers. Red means: 'looking for love'. Purple means: 'attached but open to suggestion' – i.e. 'untrustworthy in a relationship'. White means: 'Sod off you weirdo, I'm just here to buy some bread and I've got a rape alarm. I mean it.'

Although the Asda ribbon system has cleared away much of the confusion, precisely where to position yourself in the shop remains a fraught affair. Asda (Princess Way, Burnley) stocks every item imaginable that can be reproduced in an 'Asda Everyday Basics' version containing nothing but sawdust and metal. So pick your spot. Men idling in the tampon section may get the chance to meet many women, but the odds are against him coming across as someone they would want to take a Venice mini-break with.

Alternatively, repeatedly returning to the condom shelf and stuffing your trolley to overflowing with sexual lubricant might send a signal of potency, but also that you may need a quick trip to the pharmacy counter in three to four weeks' time. Magazines such as *Top Gear* show that you are into literature and the practicalities of modern transport, therefore indicating that you have both intellectual and practical sides. Buying *Knitting Monthly* and *She's Having a Baby* shows you will understand what she wants out of life.

Women looking for men should go nowhere near the fresh vegetables section. The frozen ready meals and engine oil areas are a much better bet – every guy there is single and either has a car or is very, very kinky. Girls into the edgy sort should look out for men with a bottle of Dr Pepper in their basket. Vimto is just too much. They're wrong'uns. If they have cleaning products in the basket, they are trying to look inconspicuous while shoplifting.

If you do spot someone you like, Burnley ladies should keep it subtle. Grab a French stick and lick it slowly while making eye contact with your beau. Put it in your mouth and don't break eye contact while slowly moving it in and out. If this doesn't break the ice ... well just keep going. Eventually it will.

Men can show off their alpha-male driving skills conducting their trolley through a chicane of Weetabix boxes. For added fun, try emptying a bag of ice and some frozen peas onto the surface to re-create difficult winter conditions. Or place a bunch of large bananas in front of your groin, and laugh as you look at them, saying: 'Not even close are you guys?'

Don't make jokes about melons.

Your choice of cereal is also a message. Bran flakes suggest dependable family types concerned about the health of their bowels. If you're buying Fruit Loops you obviously live on the edge and no one will be able to tell what crazy scheme you'll get up to next. If you buy a Kellogg's Variety Pack, then you like a bit of everything. Nudge nudge. Know what I mean?

> **A DISGUSTING TOWN WITH VILLAS AND SLUMS AND READY-MADE CLOTHES SHOPS.**
>
> Evelyn Waugh on Birmingham

CRAP DAYS OUT FROM THE RECENT PAST:
LOUIS TUSSAUD'S
WAX MUSEUM

'Where are we going, mum?'

'We're going for a fantastic day out at Louis Tussaud's Wax Museum in Blackpool.'

'Don't you mean Madame Tussauds Wax Museum in London?'

'Get in the car.'

> " KINDA SLEAZY. "
>
> Bill Clinton on Blackpool

TOP TEN:
BRITAIN'S
STUPIDEST TOWN

An extraordinarily unscientific survey by the quiz show *QI* recently found that Swindon was the dimmest conurbation in the whole country. Nice one Swindon. So if you fancy a really depressing day out, head over to Swindon for a chat with the locals about the important issues of the day.

The show asked 50 people in each town the following questions. The answers below are the (surprisingly) correct answers, not those the locals gave.

Q: How many legs does an octopus have?

A: Two. It has eight tentacles but only two are for walking on. The rest are for, you know, other things.

Q: Which came first, the chicken or the egg?

A: The egg. Because birds evolved from reptiles, a reptile would have laid an egg out of which the first 'official' bird would have emerged.

Q: What is paper money made from?

A: Cotton or linen.

Q: What colour are oranges?

A: Some types are orange, some are green (even when ripe).

Q: On what day should you open the first window of an advent calendar?

A: The fourth Sunday before Christmas, which can be in November or December.

Q: How would you measure the weight of your head?

A: Your head is about as dense as water, so the easiest way

is to put your head in a bucket of water and weigh the displaced water.

If you do fancy committing fraud or such, the towns which came bottom of the heap in the intelligence stakes are listed below:

10) Liverpool

9) Brighton

8) Newcastle

7) Blackpool

6) Carlisle

5) Cowdenbeath

4) Portsmouth

3) Middlesbrough

2) Birmingham

1) Swindon

David Chambers, who acted as chief quizmaster for the survey, said: 'In terms of gross stupidity, Swindon is a clear winner. When we asked the octopus question, you wouldn't believe the answers we got. How many animals have got 13 legs?'

ROMAN CHESTER
CHESHIRE

The description 'important in Roman times' is one that damns by faint praise, like 'huge in Sweden', or 'pretty fast for a Paralympian'. And as the heart sinks at the thought of the journey to Chester and the awful weather when you arrive, it sinks still further at the realisation that the city is the location for teen soap opera *Hollyoaks*; a TV show charting the beginning of the end of Western civilisation.

Still, we can't just spend the bank holiday indoors relaxing – for some reason – so it's off to Chester in the hope that the trip might not be worse than a day at the office.

Chester owes its origins to the ancient Romans, who established the military settlement of Deva at the mouth of the river Dee 2,000 years ago, doubtless in the hope that some two millennia later, lots of huffing, puffing teenagers in garish clothing might dedicate their lives to hair products, fake tan and exclaiming 'yeah – wahever!' every 74 seconds while texting people standing next to them and taking stuff which doesn't belong to them.

Also constructed as a bulwark against the warlike tribes that threatened to the west – now known as Scousers – Chester is the site of a large Roman fortress. Most of this lies underground, uselessly, but there is just enough above the surface for the tourist board to make a much bigger deal of it than by rights it should.

Anyway, if your interests occupy that slim cross-over on a Venn diagram that has one circle for 'Roman remains', another for 'soap operas about pissy northern teenagers', and a third for 'spending your few precious days off doing things you will regret', then Chester is the place for you.

Your tour/waste of an afternoon begins at the city walls,

which comprise the most complete set of town walls in Britain. Also offering a fine view of the city's actually quite attractive cathedral, the walk-about around the city walls will take approximately an hour, after which – both literally and metaphorically – it's all downhill from there. All of it.

The next best thing in Chester is its Roman amphitheatre, which is situated next to a garden dotted with Roman columns and other remains, and makes for a nice place to sit down and enjoy a picnic if, contrary to the lessons of history, it is warm and sunny. And if you're still in the mood for learning about Chester's Roman history after lunch – and frankly, you had better be – Grosvenor Museum houses the major archaeological finds of the area.

These include a large number of tombstones that helped contribute greatly to our understanding of the history of the city; and which we can confidently describe as no less interesting to see in person than they would be to read about in a book.

After that, you might try seeing if you could change your tickets for an earlier train or you could try visiting The Rows, a series of covered galleries that date back to the thirteenth century.

These impressive two-storey arcades are the High-Middle-Ages' answer to the modern-day shopping centre, and boast the same range of high street fashion names as in your own high street, so you can come to Chester and feel right at home because there is no discernible difference.

But if you've come seeking a *Hollyoaks*-based experience, then with its large number of teenagers having hissy fits dressed as footballers and impregnating each other's girlfriends, half an hour in The Rows should fit your bill.

THE OLD HOUSE OF KEYS
DOUGLAS
ISLE OF MAN

The Isle of Man's mini-parliament was once housed in this small building. Now the sign outside tells you that you can come in to 'See Touch Look Hear Learn Enjoy'. It must hint at something by listing 'see' and 'look' as separate aspects of your visit. Perhaps something of a sparseness of things to do – once you have finished 'seeing' something, you can then move on to 'looking' at it. It is uncertain whether the process is reversible – i.e., once you have then finished 'looking' at something, can you go back to 'seeing' it? Or would that screw up the time and space, like if you go back to 1935 and kill your own grandfather? Perhaps we're getting ahead of ourselves a bit here.

First up in the Old House of Keys bonanza, children have the privilege of taking a seat 'in the finely restored debating chamber'. Only, when you come to think about it, what they are doing is sitting down. Really, that's it – sitting down. It's not even an interesting room; it's just a room like any other. Most people have rooms in their own homes. So the kids are sitting down, on chairs, in a room. And you know how much that fires children's imagination. No doubt the Isle of Man youth are often at a loss for ways to fill their time other than dreaming they had been born elsewhere, but that's no excuse for offering them the chance to sit down and then dressing it up as a leisure activity.

But then comes the good bit as they must 'Listen carefully as Mr Speaker demands "Order".' That's a real high point. Listening to a man saying 'Order'. It's almost as good as when your dad says it. Or a stranger on a bus.

Sadly for disabled children, there is wheelchair access.

THE BEATLES STORY
LIVERPOOL

If there is anyone more keen to cash in on their association with the Beatles than John Lennon's wife it is The Beatles Story, a museum exploring the Fab Four's lives, music and subsequent retail opportunities.

Located in Liverpool, a city where the group formed before resorting to a contract in Hamburg in order to escape, the museum's tourist literature promises the visitor 'a magical mystery tour' – geddit? – 'to see how four young lads from Liverpool were propelled to the dizzy heights of worldwide fame and fortune to become the greatest band of all time.'

The tour is narrated by Julia Baird, John Lennon's very famous half-sister and the nearest the museum could get to involvement from the band. Baird offers such revelations along the way as that the band had numerous popular singles and led to the craze known as 'Beatlemania'. Apparently, there were 'four' of them in the band.

And if the kids aren't already sick of hearing about their dad's favourite group, then the Discovery Zone offers them the opportunity to paint a Beatles-inspired picture. Or to play a Beatles tune on a giant piano. Or create their own newspapers – activities at best tenuously linked with the Fab Four, but also closely linked to selected areas of the National Curriculum, meeting Ofsted approval as 'educational', so the museum can be a destination for lucrative school trips.

After all that Beatles-based education, it's time for a trip to the exciting-sounding Fab4D experience. Disappointingly, however, the 4D experience doesn't actually allow the visitor to travel through time as the name suggests. Instead, it's a film about the band made using 3D animation, with the absence of that fourth dimension never really explained.

What it might refer to, however, is that the Fab4D experience isn't shown in the same venue, requiring you to leave the Beatles Experience's Albert Dock building for another one at Pier Head. It might not be time travel, but it does involve travel, which takes time.

However, whether it's the Albert Dock or Pier Head, both sites embody the Beatles' mantra that 'all you need is love' by offering the chance to buy loads and loads of Beatles stuff in return for money. The Fab4Store branch at the Albert Dock presents one of the largest collections of official Beatles crap in the world, selling a range of posters, music, artwork and ill-advised clothing choices, while the branch at Pier Head offers the chance to buy more.

If you honestly haven't had enough, the city's Chavasse Park has a six-metre Peace & Harmony monument dedicated to Lennon's memory, which gives visitors the opportunity to celebrate Lennon's life and his work to promote peace by staying in bed and talking to reporters in an expensive hotel while his wife baked bread.

Speaking of expensive hotels, don't forget to visit the four-star The Hard Day's Night in the city centre, where you can go snowblind amid the Lennon Suite's gleaming white 'Imagine'-era stylings; or enjoy a relaxing night in the McCartney Suite under Macca's unblinking stare from the giant portraits of him on every wall.

SELLAFIELD NUCLEAR POWER STATION
CUMBRIA

A trip to Britain's biggest concentration of nuclear explosions sounds good, but disappoints on a truly atomic scale. What you really want to visit is the secret section where they clone sheep and make radioactive spiders bite people so they can climb up walls without ropes; but these areas are now off-limits, due to the professional killjoys from Health and Safety.

In recent years visitors to Sellafield have tailed off, probably as SPECTRE has moved into running motorway service station restaurants and mobile phone contracts.

With all the good bits hidden away, things that you are more likely to encounter are:

- A lecture theatre showing boring documentaries on the history of Sellafield, without dwelling on the time in 1957 when it all went up in flames
- Pricey catering facilities
- Pastel prints on the walls, especially chosen for their blandness
- No laser guns
- A helicopter landing pad, but it is unlikely to be used for an airborne assault while you are there

So when you get right down to it, a visit to Sellafield is just a trip to a factory, and no more exciting than if it were turning out chicken ready meals. In fact, it's a factory where you are not allowed to see the production process or the finished products. You can use the finished product when you go home and turn on a light, but that's the closest you are getting.

Kids who have been raised in what is now the traditional

family – i.e. left at home all day watching TV while mum goes to her swingers' club and dad plots the downfall of Western civilisation – will know what goes on in a real nuclear power station, like the one Homer Simpson works in. And they won't be impressed by this sanitised version.

HAWORTH, HOME TO THE BRONTËS
YORKSHIRE

Haworth, the hillside hamlet where the Brontës spent their lives, has rabidly tenuous links to the literary sisters coming out of its freezing, rain-sodden ears.

The Brontë Weaving Shed, for instance, promotes itself as very much the kind of weaving shed the Brontë sisters would have been into, had they been into weaving sheds – so much so, that it is perfectly acceptable to suggest it is, indeed, the Brontës' own weaving shed. Having set foot within the establishment in question, we would beg to differ.

Allow us to explain why.

The Brontë Weaving Shed is, undoubtedly, a shop. Anyone taking a contrary position would be very hard-pressed to make a case. The signs of being a shop are everywhere – the shelves displaying items for sale, the blatant pricing information on the goods, the tills in front of people pressing them and receiving money in exchange for goods. A distant cousin of the Edinburgh Woollen Mill (which lives in exile in England), it sells goods designed – in some cases perfectly adequately designed – to keep you warm when it's a bit chilly out. However, it has nothing, absolutely nothing, to do with Emily, Anne or Charlotte Brontë. It has even less to do with *Wuthering Heights* or *Jane Eyre*, so don't even ask.

No doubt the sisters wore clothes – there is documentary evidence that they did so – but there is little chance that they produced them in the Brontë Weaving Shed. Especially since it appears to date from the late 1980s, some 150 years after all three dropped their final stitch.

If you do pop in, you have the opportunity to pick up something pricey made out of 'The famous Brontë Tweed'.

The use of the word 'famous' must be stretching it by anybody's definition.

You can pick 'The famous Brontë Tweed' off the shelf next to the Yard of Shortbread, which meets all your metre-long biscuit needs. But don't overlook the Brontë phone sock and dangler. It's a real must. Whatever it is. But whatever it is, it's very unlikely any of the Brontës had one.

And don't think that once you step out of the shop to breathe God's sweet air, you have got away from the Brontëmania. When visiting Haworth you can stay in the Brontë Caravan Park, presumably using the Brontë sinks and toilets and experiencing Brontë regrets you didn't do something else less Brontë. For lunch you can eat in – we kid you not – the Brontë Balti House. If just visiting for the day, you can park your car in the Brontë Village Car Park, where the sisters no doubt left their Brontë cars. From their surviving letters and diaries Emily is known to have driven a Brontë Mondeo. Anne had environmental concerns and owned a hybrid-fuel Toyota Prius. Charlotte couldn't give a toss and always drove a dirty Brontë bus running on leaded petrol.

FERRY 'CROSS THE MERSEY
LIVERPOOL

Can you possibly guess which popular song is on repeat play as you wind your way on a cruise along the North's least picturesque river? That's right it's 'I Want To Fuck You Like An Animal' by Nine Inch Nails.

Only joking. It's really 'Me So Horny' by 2 Live Crew.

Nowadays the 'Ferry 'Cross the Mersey' that Gerry and The Pacemakers so loved from their base in London has morphed into a river cruise – a bit like a romantic trip along the Seine through Paris on a car ferry populated by people on their way to sign on and then steal from Asda. Yes, the post-industrial North-West, too, is for lovers.

Just remember: Liverpool's base state is 'drizzle'. If there are two dry days in a month the locals think that something must have happened. Spending five hours on a ferry in the rain as you sail past police in running battles with mobs of feral teenagers armed to the teeth isn't most people's idea of a day to cherish. Perhaps it's Gerry's, but for some reason he isn't seen on the ferry that much these days.

I TOOK A TRAIN TO LIVERPOOL. THEY WERE HAVING A FESTIVAL OF LITTER WHEN I ARRIVED.

Bill Bryson

WORLD VIKING LONGBOAT RACING CHAMPIONSHIP
PEEL
ISLE OF MAN

Looking back on pillage as a bit of a laugh is the order of the day at the World Viking Longboats Championship, as the Vikings' other favourite pastime – rape – remains controversial even to this day.

These days, the championship focuses on racing from the harbour mouth into the bay and back, rather than brutally murdering the indigenous people. Vikings come from all over their native lands – Peterborough, St Ives, Wolverhampton – to mass for this celebration of what was once hilarious barbaric destruction of lives and property in a tax haven.

But like the original British tours by insane drunken Nordics, it's probably a lot more fun to be a participant than a spectator.

Since the boaters only nip down to the bay and back wearing matching T-shirts and sensible amounts of sun-block, you can't help but think any real Viking would be a bit annoyed at how girly modern-day impersonators are. If they went the whole hog and smashed up a couple of churches that would be a spectacle.

Given that their frequent unexpected presence was, at best, something of a mixed blessing for the population of north-east England during the Dark Ages, Vikings seem strangely popular these days. But of course women famously love a bastard, and who deserves the term more?

If anyone in Peel has forgotten there is a Viking longboat festival coming, opening their curtains in the morning might be a bit of a worrying experience.

THE SWITCHING ON OF THE BLACKPOOL ILLUMINATIONS
BLACKPOOL

The lights display is a curious British tradition. Rather like inviting your friends round to see you flick the switch in your bathroom, it is literally no more than the turning on of a number of electric bulbs – with all the wonder that holds for a 21st-century audience.

No doubt Thomas Edison felt pretty chuffed when he showed his glowing orb to all and sundry, but in the hundred years since then, most of us in the Western world have got pretty used to being able to read after the sun has gone to beddy-byes.

Yet, in stark defiance of modern society's *ennui de lightbulb*, every August the otherwise bleak and windswept Lancashire coast town of Blackpool plays host to one of the least amazing shows the world has ever known.

Even the town's choice of when to run the lights is an odd one, beginning at the end of August and running to early November – i.e. after most visitors have gone home. This means that after the first couple of days it is so cold that the only way to see the lights is from inside a car while wearing a parka jacket, generally resulting in a slew of attractively lit traffic accidents as drivers look up at the lights, not the other cars or the screaming pedestrians with their faces pressed against the windscreen.

Still, you have to feel a bit sorry for Blackpool. A hundred-odd years ago it was deliriously exciting for the factory workers of Lancashire to be presented with a town where they could acquire a fish supper, a kiss-me-quick hat and herpes within 24 hours of arrival. But this glamour has definitely faded. Now you can go for days without developing a single sexually transmitted disease.

In an effort to inject some TV glamour into the event, Blackpool's Illuminations committee even recently hired TV interior designer and surprise heterosexual Laurence Llewelyn-Bowen to design one of the exhibits. Blackpool being in the north of England and bastion of working-class men-are-men attitudes, you do have to wonder what was going through their minds when they hired a long-haired wallpaper and lamp specialist who dresses like an eighteenth-century dandy.

Don't get us wrong – we're all in favour of lights, and electric lights definitely seem the way to go. It's just that making them into a tourist attraction when we can get the same effect by opening a fridge door is never going to be a winner.

> **A SAD PLACE THAT HAS LOST ITS HEART ... YET VISITORS SEEM HAPPY AS THEY STAGGER FROM ONE DRINKING PLACE TO ANOTHER PICKING THEIR WAY AROUND POOLS OF URINE AND VOMIT THAT APPEAR ON THE STREETS AFTER DARK.**
>
> Lib Dem MP Adrian Saunders on Blackpool

PENDLE WITCHES TRAIL
LANCASHIRE

No boast about one's visitor attraction could express less self-confidence than the boast that you can experience it without having to leave the car. And so it is with the Pendle Witches Trail, which offers a faster, automotive alternative for those that might decide not to bother if the trip involved standing up.

The car trail – during which you need never leave the warm, safe environment of your Ford Focus where nothing can hurt you or ever make you unhappy again – introduces you to some of the places mentioned in the historical accounts of the Pendle Witch Trial of 1612, England's biggest (and best!) ever trial for witchcraft, which concluded in the hanging of no fewer than ten brides of Beelzebub.

With both a multiple hanging and witches, Pendle has two good ingredients for a creepy gothic day out; particularly for those who enjoyed Vincent Price in *Witchfinder General*. But if there is one major flaw about witches where automobile-based tourism is concerned, it is that they didn't contribute much in the way of architecture, or even artefacts. This is because they are not conquering armies, great artists or religious leaders, but the seventeenth-century equivalent of people locally rumoured to be paedophiles.

So although Pendle was the scene of the most significant witch trial in British history, it looks very much like somewhere that wasn't, but was the scene of a bit of farming and some cottage industries such as butter production. But the fact that there isn't actually much witch-related stuff to see or do isn't going to hold back the local tourist board, which is determined to make a Lucifer-based attraction of the place come hell or high water. Preferably both.

The not-quite-worth-parking-for tour begins at the Pendle

Heritage Centre in Barrowford, which has a wealth of information about the Pendle Witches that you could have read at home, sitting down with a cat. The centre is also the start and end point for the Pendle Way, a nice little walking route that, while very pleasant, sadly has no witch-based excitement of any kind.

Next on the trail is the village of Hoarstones, where on All Hallows' Eve in 1633, a boy claimed he was held prisoner by witches. The boy named 17 of his alleged captors, who in a greedy second round of Lancashire witch-purging were gaoled after trials in 1633–4, then was sent to London as a sort of a witch-based travelling circus to remind people in the south how the north isn't old-fashioned in a quaint and friendly way like on an advert for Hovis bread, but in more of a harsh and backward, they-hang-little-old-ladies-for-owning-brooms sort of a way.

Anyway, is there any trace of the boy or the trial to be found at Hoarstones? Anything to see? Even a plaque? No. So no need to even look up from the satnav.

Following the prescribed route past a series of pubs, an art gallery and a couple of other places that don't have anything to do with witches but at which one might put some cash into the local economy, the Routefinder General eventually arrives at Ashlar House, where accused witches were interrogated and sent for trial. Woooh – could be eerie. But it's a private house and you can't go in. So no need for the handbrake here, just keep driving.

Taking the turning past St Johns church, you will enter the village of Higham, where a witch and several of her supposed victims, who were probably just faking it for a laugh, lived. Witch-based points of interest? The Four Alls Inn, which has 'an interesting sign and a stone horse trough'. Spooky!

And so it continues, past the home of local best-named

witch Alice Nutter, which is another private house that you can't enter and where your car won't be possessed; past the uncanny Barley Picnic Site with its spooky toilets and unearthly information point; past the evil Pendle Inn; past the ungodly Barley Mow restaurant and … on to the sinister Barley Tearooms.

If you have time, you might want to park the old broomstick at Pendle Hill, which is where George Fox founded the Quaker movement, and which has a lovely view of the surrounding countryside and not a single witch-related thing. Or just carry on to the M65.

> **WHAT A PITY IT IS THAT WE HAVE NO AMUSEMENTS IN ENGLAND BUT VICE AND RELIGION.**
>
> Sidney Smith

TOP TEN:
ATTRACTIONS WITH NAMES THAT JUST INVITE RIDICULE

1) The National Space Centre, Snibston Discovery Park, Leicestershire

How exciting! A special centre dedicated to learning all about the prestigious British space programme, the British moon landing and the country's long rivalry with the Soviet space programme. Oh.

Yes, the National Space Centre in Leicestershire tracks the proud history of all of the exploration of space that Britain never took part in. With six hands-on galleries allowing you to do stuff like test-drive a Rover Robot which no one from Britain will do for real, as well as a 360-degree planetarium that shows you all the places British people won't be going without a lift from the Americans, it's actually not a bad day out, especially if you have kids. But its use of the word 'national' is as misleading as it would be at the UK's National Hoverboard Centre, or Britain's National Centre of Disneyland in Florida.

2) Much Wenlock, Shropshire

OK, so the Shropshire town of Much Wenlock could be a worse place for a visit, with its medieval buildings, sixteenth-century guildhall and ruins of a priory sacked by Danish invaders in the ninth century. It's just that its name simply raises the question: how much Wenlock would a Wenlock lock if a Wenlock could lock Wen?

How much Wenlock? Much Wenlock (etc., etc.).

3) National Fishing Heritage Centre, Grimsby, Lincolnshire

What's more boring than fishing? Oh, a museum about fishing. OK, OK, it's the out-on-the-open-sea kind, not the sitting-by-the-canal-drinking-tea-from-a-Thermos kind, but while that is marginally more exciting to do, it's not a whole lot more exciting to learn about. The centrepiece depicts the 1950s heyday of the distant waters fishing fleet. We'll leave it there because something might be on the telly.

4) Monkey World Ape Rescue Centre, Wareham, Dorset

Dorset's Monkey World Ape Rescue Centre provides the chance to visit furry friends that have been rescued from sad lives spent sitting about smoking fags for postcards or being kicked in the ribs as part of the Albanian tourist industry. What it doesn't do, alas, is provide a fourth emergency service. Why bother with the fire brigade when the Ape Rescue team could have your cat out of that tree in half the time? Kids' party entertainer failing to hold the attention of the little ones? Tea bag ad campaign flagging? You would know who to call. And 999 Rescue would be SO MUCH better a TV show.

5) Offa's Dyke Centre, Powys, Wales

Offa's Dyke Centre takes its name from the giant rampart built by Offa, an eighth-century King of Mercia, who ruled over a large area of central England. An uncompromising ruler and an effective administrator, Offa used every opportunity to consolidate his territory, in this case by constructing a giant rampart to divide his kingdom from Powys to the west. But the museum still sounds like a poorly named outreach project run by one of Britain's more left-wing local authorities.

6) The London Brass Rubbing Centre.

Enough said. Actually, no, hang on, does anything else think this sounds like a sexual technique? Anyone? Oh, right.

7) The Birmingham International Airport Visitor Centre

Experience the thrill of landing at Birmingham International Airport or simply re-live that great, just-checked-in-now-looking-at-stuff-and-waiting-to-board feeling at the Birmingham International Airport Visitor Centre. The centre, conveniently located next to Arrivals and now having given up on charging admission, also provides information on other local attractions and events. See you there!

Wait – where are you going? It's this way! Hey!

8 Willis Museum of Basingstoke Town and Country Life, Hampshire

The Willis Museum of Basingstoke Town and Country Life offers perhaps the narrowest purview of any museum in Britain. Everything you have ever wanted to know about town or country life in Basingstoke can be found inside, with local history and up-to-date information about the UK home of Sun Life Financial, Motorola and the BNP Paribas Lease Group UK. And absolutely no information about those bastards in Reading and Winchester next door.

9) Robin Hood's Ball

A Neolithic causeway on Salisbury Plain but you have to admit it sounds a lot like a testicle that robs from the rich and gives to the poor.

10) Jodrell Bank Science Centre & Arboretum, Lower Withington, Cheshire

The Jodrell Bank Science Centre & Arboretum is part of the Jodrell Bank Centre for Astrophysics at the University of Manchester, which has played an important role in the research of meteors, quasars, pulsars and gravitational lenses, as well as having been heavily involved in the tracking of probes at the start of the space age. But Jodrell Bank still sounds like rhyming slang.

'Hurry up in the bathroom, will you? I'm going to be late for work.'

'Sod off, I'm having a Jodrell.'

> **LORD CHIEF JUSTICE: 'WHERE LAY THE KING LAST NIGHT?'**
> **GOWER: 'AT BASINGSTOKE, MY LORD.'**
> **LORD CHIEF JUSTICE: 'I HOPE, MY LORD, ALL'S WELL?'**
>
> Shakespeare, *Henry IV Part 2*

WORLD BLACK PUDDING THROWING CHAMPIONSHIP
RAMSBOTTOM
LANCASHIRE

There is a difference between the endearing tradition-maintaining silly types who throw themselves suicidally after cheeses thrown down hills in the Cooper's Hill Cheese Rolling and Wake (as people have been doing for hundreds of years), and the bores who design their own wackiness in order that they can say 'I'm mad, me!' to people curling their toes up inside their shoes in awkwardness. The first are sufferable, the second most certainly are not. The entrants into the council-run World Black Pudding Throwing Championship fall squarely in the second camp.

For hours they throw the black puddings at a stack of Yorkshire puddings behind a pub with the aim of knocking some off. Black puddings are, of course, large blood clots, and this must therefore also rank as one of the least sanitary activities one can perform outside an Oldham brothel.

Sure, there are parts of Lancashire which have so completely run out of ideas for ways to put themselves on the map that chucking semi-edible congealed blood around outside the town's popular off-licence is the only option left, but that doesn't mean we have to applaud while they do it.

As previous champion pudding thrower John Burns said, 'It feels a bit ridiculous to be honest.'

THE CAT POTTERY
WENSLEYDALE
YORKSHIRE

There's something a bit creepy about the Cat Pottery, which ... well ... displays pottery about cats. Inside the pottery and outside in the garden, everywhere you look, ceramic and stone cats stare at you, as if they're sizing you up for nightfall. And just wait until you see the cat graveyard. You won't sleep.

> **ON A FINE DAY THE CLIMATE OF ENGLAND IS LIKE LOOKING UP A CHIMNEY, ON A FOUL DAY IT IS LIKE LOOKING DOWN.**
>
> Anonymous

CUMBERLAND PENCIL MUSEUM
KESWICK

As any parent knows, teenagers are obsessed with pencils. They can't get enough of the things. What don't they like? An internet connection and a lack of parental supervision. What do they like? Pencils.

Pencils. Pencils. Pencils. Sometimes pens.

Luckily, all their stationery-related dreams can come true at the Cumberland Pencil Museum, based in an old pencil factory. 'Home of the world's first pencil!' We didn't put that exclamation mark in, they did. Because that claim really deserves an exclamation mark, in the way that, say, 'We've put a bomb under your car!' or 'Help me!' deserves one.

The Cumberland Pencil Museum's greatest attraction is, undoubtedly, the World's Longest Pencil, which comes in at an amazing eight metres. It's a whopper all right.

Presumably, the Cumberland pencil is the 'World's Longest' because nobody was interested in producing one which is longer. At least when Edmund Hillary and Sherpa Tenzing dragged themselves to the top of the world's tallest mountain they had quite a nice view to look forward to, or when some Spanish village gets together to make the world's biggest jug of sangria they have one mental street party. But when you finally get to see the World's Longest Pencil all you see is a normal pencil, only bigger. You can get the same effect by taking a normal-sized pencil and putting your eyes really close to it. The Big Pencil is so useless you can't even write with it, unless you have an equally enormous piece of paper and giant hands. And even then it would still be rubbish because you still have to find an utterly massive desk to keep it in.

Still, the big pencil isn't the only thing to see at the Cumberland Pencil Museum, which also boasts 'great resources for schools and colleges'. One can only presume they have a room dedicated to the pencil's application in pornography and drinking cider. What this would be is unclear.

If that isn't enough, the feral youth will no doubt be calmed by looking at the other treasures in the Pencil Museum. For instance the embarrassment of riches in the Pencil Registry, which is the order book from the old pencil factory around which the museum is based. After all, who wouldn't be fascinated by endless lists of the names and addresses of people who once bought some pencils? As much fun as reading the phone directory. Next to a big pencil.

SHEFFIELD

When The Full Monty hit British cinemas in 1997, the residents of Sheffield, where it was set, were outraged at the depiction of their town as some depressed, poverty-stricken slum populated by overweight former steelworkers living in hovels with outside toilets. Their anger was justified because Sheffield is far worse than that.

Under an ever-present atmosphere of imminent assault, more than half a million souls are crammed within its borders like a giant open prison. Mary Queen of Scots was held under house arrest in Sheffield for 14 years. She must have dreaded the day they let her out.

Supposedly, Sheffield natives are known to the people from nearby towns as 'Dee-dahs' – short for 'Lah-dee-dahs', suggesting, far beyond the capacity for human comprehension, that they are posh. As Lord Justice Lawton once said: 'Wife beating may be socially acceptable in Sheffield, it is a different matter in Cheltenham.'

The Sheffield Bus Museum liked the city so much it moved to Rotherham.

> **EVEN WIGAN IS BEAUTIFUL COMPARED WITH SHEFFIELD.**
> George Orwell

CRINKLEY BOTTOM THEME PARK
MORECAMBE
LANCASHIRE

A cautionary tale to all who would mess with the dark forces of low-quality BBC light entertainment. For eight years of state-sponsored hell, Noël Edmonds subjected the public to *Noel's House Party*, a show that made an episode of *Sooty* look like heavyweight political debate.

The show, which was set in Edmonds's fictional house in the fictional village of Crinkley Bottom, was a real-life vehicle for Edmonds's fictional talent. But Edmonds wasn't happy with hurting the millions of people who had no access to such simple pleasures as 'books' or 'turning the TV off when that smug bleached-blond git comes on'. Like Robespierre, he wanted to take the terror onto the streets.

Thus Edmonds opened the Crinkley Bottom park in the seaside town of Morecambe, Lancashire. It opened in summer 1994 – a towering reflection of Edmonds's talent. And closed in autumn 1994 because no one wanted to go there – a towering reflection of Edmonds's unpopularity.

Morecambe's Edmonds-themed dystopia was actually one of three Crinkley Bottoms, the other two being rebrandings of existing failed parks. They quickly reverted to their older status, preferring to die with honour than live a life of shame in association with Edmonds.

Just why the public stayed away from Crinkley Bottom in their droves is almost inexplicable. But hell, we'll give it a whirl. Perhaps it was the fact that Mr Blobby, the parks' mascot, was actually dreamed up on the TV series to be the embodiment of a stomach-churningly vapid children's character. Perhaps it was the fact that children aged six months old felt it was a little immature. But it was probably Edmonds himself – after all, he did insist on turning up from time to time.

After the Morecambe park closed, losing the local council millions of pounds in a disaster amusingly dubbed 'Blobbygate' by the local press, there was an official report into who was to blame. Never one for self-aggrandisement, Edmonds actually said: 'We wanted these people investigated because they cheated the people of Morecambe out of something that could have been very significant. I always thought Morecambe was famous for shrimps, it's now notorious for fudge.'

Still, better than being known for a bastard-themed tourist attraction.

In 1996, someone set fire to the shuttered remnants of the park. Like swearing, arson is never 'big' nor 'clever'. Except when it is.

"THE ENGLISHMAN IS NEVER CONTENT BUT WHEN HE IS GRUMBLING."

Scottish saying

DELTA FORCE PAINTBALL
WAKEFIELD

Paintballing is a mainstay of the corporate team-bonding scene. Where once office workers resorted to shagging on the desks at the Christmas party to cement their business relationships, the same function is now performed by trying to shoot each other in the face. That's progress.

There's nothing like spending an afternoon in the company of someone who wishes he had served in Vietnam, with all the unusual opportunities that would have brought him. So to help you along the way, Delta Force Paintball has recreated a Viet Cong village which you can storm – presumably wiping out anyone who happens to be passing by at the time and then torching the place to make sure it doesn't fall into enemy hands. All in some woods near Wakefield.

You will find that it's always the quiet ones who go utterly staring-eyed mental in these events. It will be Clive from Purchasing who runs out of paintballs halfway through and resorts to ambushing you with a nail-studded club, dropping on you from the trees or rising out of a pile of leaves to beat you unconscious from behind while 'The Ride Of The Valkyries' plays in his head. From there he will strip you naked and suspend your lifeless body from the trees as a warning to others, before making himself a new set of clothing from animal furs reinforced with tree bark. You should have noticed the signs when he started talking to himself in the office.

'Where's Clive?' they will ask on Monday morning.

'He went sort of … feral,' you will explain.

'Will he be back?'

'I don't think so.'

TOP TEN:
MOST TENUOUS
HISTORICAL CONNECTIONS

1) Ware, Hertfordshire
The Great Bed of Ware is this village's claim to fame. It is a bed which is larger than average like the ones very fat people have made. Now in the Victoria and Albert Museum in London, it is nowhere near Ware.

2) Hastings, East Sussex
The Battle of Hastings was fought at the town of Battle. It is miles away from Hastings … but does share the town's problems of social deprivation.

3) The Lost Gardens of Heligan, Cornwall
They are well signposted and the website gives full driving directions. Not quite the Hanging Gardens of Babylon or the Lost Temple of the Incas. More like that restaurant you remember going to and it takes you a few minutes to find the address.

4) American Adventure Park, Ilkeston, Derbyshire
Recreating Derbyshire's place in the history of the Wild West.

5) Rob Roy and Trossachs Visitor Centre, Stirlingshire
Trossachs has stolen a march on its rival attractions by declaring itself as the capital of 'Rob Roy Country'. Sure, Callander might be bereft of any visible historical remains or connection to the man, but then where exactly is Rob Roy country anyway? Ah, here it is, in a converted church near the coach stop.

6) Robin Hood Leisure Park, Leicestershire

In fairness, Robin Hood Leisure Park doesn't even try to justify its name. But we're sure the Prince of Thieves would have made merry at the park's Club Tropicana venue, where affordable family entertainment for 2011 included guest appearances from The Four Tops and TV's Keith Harris & Orville, who still remember the good times.

7) The Cavern Club, Liverpool

Not the one the Beatles played at. That was demolished in the 1970s. This is a pretend version.

8) Blackpool Dinosaur Safari

Big plastic models.

9) National Football Museum, Preston

Located in the stadium of the mighty Preston North End who were in the Football League in 1889, thus justifying their claim to host a national museum far more than anyone else.

10) Museum of Antiquities, Newcastle

Boasts that it includes models of Hadrian's Wall, models of Roman soldiers and a model of the Temple Of Mithras.

HADRIAN'S WALL
NORTHUMBERLAND

It's insulting enough to the Scots that after conquering most of Europe, much of Africa and a fair chunk of the Middle East, the Romans took a quick look around Scotland and decided not to bother.

To add insult to injury the emperor Hadrian decided in AD 122 to build a wall with which to keep the Scots out, doubtless worried that without one the Scots might come down and ruin the civilised world with their excessive drinking, deep-fried confectionery and propensity for supporting 'Anyone But Rome' in the World Cup.

And just to make sure that the Caledonians felt really, really slighted, he decided to make that wall really, really, pathetically easy for any proper army not made up of men in skirts to get across.

Yes, Hadrian's Wall might be one of the supreme wall-based engineering achievements of the ancient world in that particular geographical region, but as any woman will tell you, it's not the length that counts, but the girth. And what Hadrian erected was very skinny indeed and so low it could be scaled by an asthmatic Shetland pony, given enough run-up. Insultingly minuscule. Like keeping the enemy out of your empire by removing the signs on the doors that say 'push' or 'pull'.

SCOTLAND

HOGMANAY
EDINBURGH

Edinburgh is an incredibly dramatic city. Built across a ravine gouged millennia ago by a migrating glacier, one side sitting atop an extinct volcano, the other a sweep of majestic Georgian townhouses, it is also sodding freezing in winter.

Despite this, thousands of unsuspecting English, American and Antipodean tourists flock to the city on 31 December each year believing that the 'atmosphere' will keep them warm. Actually, it is the 'atmosphere' that makes you cold.

The reason for this is quite complicated, but please stay with us on this. The reason is that Edinburgh is in Scotland. Scotland is a cold place, and winter is the coldest part of the year. Some people would go as far as to say Scotland 'has form' for being on the cooler side and winter is fast gaining a reputation for being chilly. These facts are not secrets; people discuss them openly in pubs and during tennis games with casual acquaintances. So you don't have to be a genius to work out that wearing shorts and flip-flops as the clock strikes midnight on 31 December is just going to land you in the nearest accident and emergency unit with the distinct chance of losing a toe – but then you've got nine more and what are they really there for anyway? You can't pick stuff up with them.

Anyway, the complete lack of ambient warmth is the reason all the genuine residents of Edinburgh bugger off for the holidays, wistfully shaking their heads at the scores of misled foreigners bouncing out of the trains at Waverley station, ready for their grins to be frozen off their ruddy-cheeked faces while tiny little icicles form on their eyelashes. Little do they know that because they bought the festival-style white wristband for £49.99 and not the gold wristband for £69.99 or the platinum wristband for £89.99 and one blond-haired child, they will actually be stuck in a Tesco car park closer to Berlin than to Edinburgh's picturesque Royal Mile.

For 31 December sees Edinburgh turned into a giant internment camp which the council actually charges you to enter and battery hens think is cramped. Barricades and armed police who have been drinking prevent any free-born Briton who has not paid the requisite money from walking along the streets his taxes pay to build, maintain and sweep. If the message still hasn't got through, the underfed Alsatians straining at the slipping grip of their handlers will push the point home.

A quite staggering – and we mean staggering – number of the 'revellers' have also forgotten one minor point. Yes, the celebrations go on until after midnight, but not for ever. Like happiness and the love of your first girlfriend, they come to an end much sooner than you think and you will need somewhere to sleep at some point. For many who have forgotten to call the Holiday Inn seven years in advance, this means the only bed you will be spending the night in will also have flowers growing out of it. Luckily, there is an ancient Scottish tradition of welcoming the 'first foot' – the first visitor of the new year. So the houseowner will cheerily wake you at 11am with a hot breakfast and a mug of cocoa. They most certainly won't wake you angrily at 6am with a kick to the nuts and throw stones at you as you limp down the street crying like a child. For that would be unwelcoming and therefore contrary to all the utterly mythical rules of Scottish hospitality. ('Don't worry Crispin, I speak a little Scottish and I'm sure they mean us no harm. Ow! Christ! Please, not the face!')

THE HIGHLAND GAMES
BRAEMAR

There are many things to be celebrated about the culture of East Asia, but its cutlery isn't one of them. Halfway through fashioning a wooden fork in Something BC, the region's most influential craftsman must have heard that dinner was ready, looked at the little sticks he had whittled thus far and thought 'these will do for now'.

A similar hey-ho attitude to craftsmanship could be found among the ancient Scots, who never got as far as the Greeks did in fashioning a wooden javelin for their games, and resigned themselves to throwing an entire log instead because it cut down on the work.

Tossing the caber – or as it's also known, 'javelin for the crap at woodwork' – continues to this day, and is just one of the events of the Highland Games, annual celebrations of Scottish sport and 'culture' that are held across Scotland each year as well as in Canada, the United States and other places with the waferest of wafer-thin connections to Caledonia.

The most prestigious Highland Games take place at Braemar in Scotland, attended by the Queen and her Greek husband: a crap day out for all the Royal Family to watch what are known collectively – and apparently without sarcasm – as 'Scottish heavy athletics'.

As well as the caber toss, the 'athletic' events include the Stone Put, an event similar to the modern-day Shot Put except – you guessed it – using a stone instead; the Hammer Throw, which needs no explanation; and the Sheaf Toss, which is one of the more sophisticated events in that it involves not merely throwing a bundle of straw, but throwing it over a pole.

And while none of the Heavy Athletics events involves an object it's a good idea to be chucking about in a crowd, the event that trumps them all is the Weight Throw, which dispenses with the idea of even specifying what's being chucked at all and merely points out that it has to be something heavy.

As well as the chance to see people chucking random stuff, which could never grow boring, a visit to the Games also offers the chance to see displays of traditional Scottish dancing and other bits of everyday Scots culture, such as bagpipes and displays of swordsmanship and drumming.

Needless to say, all this makes for a great day out – everyone loves the sound of bagpipes! However, if we have one complaint, it is with regards to authenticity: the Highland Games just aren't Scottish enough.

Sure, dancing, bagpipes and chucking stuff might once have represented Scottish life, but those days are long gone. For the Highland Games to really represent Scotland, they must move with the times and reflect the country as it is today.

Buckfast Downing, already a popular sport at amateur level, could become an official event. Why have displays of swordsmanship when the modern day weapon of choice is the knife, hammer or housebrick? And what could be more Scottish than a deep-frying contest?

THE BELARUS OF THE WEST.

Nial Ferguson on Scotland

ROBERT BURNS TRAIL
DUMFRIES AND GALLOWAY

Ah, Robbie Burns: the Ploughman's Poet, Scotland's Favourite Son, the Bard of Ayrshire and the creator of absolutely nothing worth visiting.

Born in 1759, Robert Burns died aged just 37 after writing poems and songs that endeared him to a nation and leaving not a single landmark of any kind worth seeing.

Burns was born near Ayr in a tiny and unremarkable house that is now the Burns Cottage museum, where you can see the small thatched roof that may have kept the rain from the poet's head if it were raining, the original wall that potentially sheltered him from the north wind, the original wall that equally possibly protected him from the east wind. And the other walls.

After living there for a bit, Burns took up a job as an excise officer in Dumfries, 47 bloody miles away, where he wrote a number of his celebrated poems and continued to eschew work as an architect, and where Burns-lovers can resume the trail after their initial disappointment.

Burns's statue there is overlooked by the unremarkable Greyfriars Church that has no connection to him, and along the high street is the Globe Inn, a pub that Burns used to drink at because he lived in Dumfries just like lots of other people. There are probably other pubs nearby that are unconnected to Robert Burns.

The Globe is full of character and miserable tourists, and contains artefacts such as a chair by the fire that he might have sat in sometimes to rest his poetic legs, perhaps while thinking of some poems and not building any form of notable landmark, and a window that features some scratches that he is said to have made with his diamond ring, perhaps while thinking of some poems.

After that it's a short, desultory walk to the great man's fairly ordinary house in Burns Street – a street almost certainly named after the poet Robbie Burns! The medium-sized house is now a comprehensive shrine to the poet, stuffed with a host of his unremarkable possessions, and may well have been the place in which he composed songs such as Scotland's unofficial national anthem, 'Auld Lang Syne', and at no point thought to create any sort of artefact or structure that would outlast him.

When you've had your fill of seeing the sorts of spoons that Robbie Burns might have used to eat soup with and the sort of bowl that the soup might have been served in – and the door handles he would have used to open the doors with using his own hands, perhaps while he was thinking up a poem – you can then stroll on to St Michael's Kirkyard, where the Burns Mausoleum can be found.

If you're still up for it, and it doesn't look like rain, you can head for the Robert Burns Centre, an old mill full of more of Burns's very ordinary possessions, plus a model of how Dumfries could have looked when he lived there, before not very extensive changes were made to the town that would render it completely recognisable to someone who had lived in Burns's time.

Assuming that the wife hasn't taken the kids' side yet, clench your jaw and press on for the final, five-mile trip to the village of Auldgirth, where the poet lived for three years. You can see his wife's kitchen there, if you want. There's a riverside path, where Burns might have walked. Or hopped. And the Hermitage, a tiny stone building where Burns sometimes slept and where you, in the 21st century, pledged never to celebrate Burns Night again.

STUDENT PLAYS AT THE
EDINBURGH FESTIVAL

If there's anything worse than students – which there isn't – it's drama students. And the annual Edinburgh Festival has bloody loads of them in one place, running around as if they weren't just terrible pockmarks on the face of humanity.

Encompassing the International Festival, the Fringe Festival, the Film Festival, the Arts Festival, the Book Festival, the Jazz Festival and the STD Festival, if it were possible to give an entire town a poke in the eye, you would.

Anyone who has been will tell you it is an unforgettable experience. What they mean is that it was an unforgivable one. With such an assault on human dignity, it is a scandal the UN has not become involved.

Whom did Johnny McStudent believe his nine-hour surreal work set in a mental asylum would entertain? Presumably people who don't like afternoons.

Of course, it's not just the writing that makes or breaks a show. The acting, directing, design and choice of venue all conspire against it too. And university drama societies are often run on professional lines, meaning that whoever is sleeping with the director at the time gets the lead role, and the next biggest goes to whoever has a car or parents with a flat in Edinburgh.

The unwritten rule of student theatre direction is that at times of great emotion, everyone must get on the floor. Rolling on it, crying on it, trying to shag it, whatever – something must be happening to the floor to really annoy the audience who can't then see you. Of course, this is only a problem if there actually is an audience – which in Edinburgh is, thankfully, a rare occurrence.

WHALE WATCHING
ISLE OF SKYE

Not so much 'whale watching' as 'seeing a black blob on the horizon and guessing that it might be a whale, or possibly a boat or a wave'.

The more unhappy Scottish islands have gone big on 'watching' unsociable distant sea creatures in recent years, as their traditional industry of wrecking passing ships in order to bludgeon the astonished survivors to death and steal their cargo has waned – a victim of our namby-pamby health-and-safety society and meddling bureaucrats from Brussels. There are now children growing up in the Orkneys who have never beaten an exhausted sailor to death with sticks. It's the end of an ancient way of life. And death.

Instead they now tempt ecology-obsessed middle-class women to drive their Range Rovers in second gear from north London to Inverness for a quick hop across the treacherous North Sea in an overloaded rowing boat. They are promised that when they arrive a friendly whale will come up to them in the charming local pub to have a bit of a chat about – oh, marine things, you know. The ethnically dressed visitors who read the *Independent* could, of course, just drive across the bridge from the mainland to Skye, but that would spoil the image for the townies that they are visiting a community which is at one with nature and doesn't know what bridges are.

Yet anyone who has actually set foot on a Scottish island will know that they are not all heather and rolling hills; they tend to be all piercing rain and repeat methadone prescriptions. It's good that the methadone is there, because it's a happy green colour; in stark contrast to the greyness of the island – grey houses, grey seas, grey skin, grey food. Not so much 'at one with nature' as 'at one with anti-depressants and long-term unemployment'.

The Islingtonites don't even need to travel to Skye to catch a glimpse of a black shadow almost visible through a telescope – they can just hang around the banks of the Thames and wait for another of the sea monsters to take a wrong turn at Gravesend and end up beside Tower Bridge looking more than a little lost as one surprised example did in 2008. The shock of being within blowhole-distance of a cockney was enough to kill it. Given the choice of watching a whale from miles away on a remote Scottish island, or watching one die in the capital, you might just be better off watching whales on telly.

And the BBC's David Attenborough has spent many hours and many thousands of pounds trying to get a good view of whales just so you don't have to, and his excellent documentaries are on almost permanent repeat on satellite TV. Forget whale watching on Skye – try whale watching on Sky.

Skye, of course, is a very historical and interesting island in its own right. It is well known for *The Skye Boat Song* about how Bonnie Prince Charlie heroically buggered off in the middle of a battle as all his followers were being slaughtered while trying to claim England's throne for the delusional Italian – you know it, you had to sing it in Music.

> *Speed, bonnie boat, like a bird on the wing,*
> *Onward! the sailors cry;*
> *Carry the lad that's born to be King*
> *Over the sea to Skye.*

Strangely, the lyrics make no mention of the fact that during his royal scarpering he was dressed as a girl because he was scared he would be recognised and might have to do some fighting for himself instead of getting unemployed people from

Glasgow to do it for him. Displaying the military prowess and bravery that has always characterised the Italian army, he realised that disappearing while dressed as a milkmaid was the best option for saving his skin while abandoning all his surprised followers whom he promised he might come back for if he had a moment. Of course, any man landing on a remote Scottish island wearing a frock is placing himself in dangers he can't even imagine.

> **THERE ARE TWO SEASONS IN SCOTLAND: JUNE AND WINTER.**
>
> Billy Connolly

TOP TEN:
UGLIEST BUILDINGS
IN BRITAIN

1) Cumbernauld Town Shopping Centre, North Lanarkshire
This was once the centrepiece of an award-winning 1960s new town near Glasgow but is now largely abandoned. Cumbernauld was named the second crappiest place to live (after Hull) by the *Idler* magazine. God help those in Hull.

2) The Imax Cinema, Bournemouth
Beware councils and developers boasting of their ability to promote regeneration. This cinema and leisure complex, which was built in the 1990s, was supposed to reinvigorate Bournemouth's waterfront. It closed after three years and is still spoiling the sea view for residents.

3) Northampton Bus Station
A 1970s behemoth that dominates an otherwise small-scale historic town.

4) Crown House, Kidderminster
Another gem from the 1960s, this once housed the Inland Revenue making both its exterior and interior unpopular.

5) The Cement Works, Rugby
The only industrial building on the list. It is the size of a cathedral and blights Rugby, according to locals. Cement: a strangely controversial material. Both gift and curse to man, how many times has a face been raised in anguish at the mixed blessing of a car parking facility and screaming-blight-on-the-landscape?

6) Gateshead Car Park

This multistorey co-starred alongside Michael Caine in the British gangster movie *Get Carter*. Many locals loathed it, but it remained loved by devotees of brutalist architecture. After *Get Carter* its career nose-dived and it was destroyed in the summer of 2010.

7) The Scottish Parliament, Edinburgh

Built ten times over budget – yes, *ten* – and three years late, but it still won the 2005 Stirling Prize for architecture.

8) The Tower, Colliers Wood

This 19-storey office block dominates a residential area of south-west London. Some 86 per cent of residents said it was the worst thing about living in the area, so it is far less popular than street crime and domestic violence.

9) Lodges Supermarket, Holmfirth

This derelict 1970s supermarket was built in the West Yorkshire town that provides the setting for sitcom *Last of the Summer Wine* and has therefore blighted the lives of people right across the country for 30 years running.

10) Number 1, Westminster Bridge

Stranded on a busy London roundabout, and empty for 20 years, it looked like a badly shuffled deck of cards. Then, finally, in 2010 it was knocked down and everyone cheered.

AMERICAN FOOTBALL IN SCOTLAND

Americans have many faults – the inability to determine appropriate food portions, for instance – but one thing they have definitely mastered is pizzazz. If what you want is flashing, glowing, sparkling things, or skimpily dressed schoolgirls doing somersaults while a dozen midgets are simultaneously blasted out of a dozen cannons and the entire audience stands to pledge allegiance to their national flag (apart from the girls' male teachers who need to keep their legs crossed and their hands in their pockets), you go to Uncle Sam to organise it. The man is a showman through and through. Just look at his hat.

What you don't do is leave it to the dour denizens of the most rain-soaked, grey-skied, Buckfast-sozzled corner of Britain. But back in the 1990s, a strange passion gripped much of the United Kingdom. We saw open-topped cars and an open-topped Pamela Anderson on TV. We thought it all looked sparkly. And Scotland even went as far as importing the national sport, sprouting American Football teams like mushrooms. Now these teams are as rare as Michelin-starred restaurants in Dundee.

Frankly, American Football is a not a great game. It stops every 12 seconds, it has no genuine skill or tactics, and the players are so afraid of getting hurt that they wear motorbike helmets. Yes, pretty much the only things American football has going for it are the twirling girls and the dwarves. And due to Political Correctness Gone Mad, they're not even allowed to use the dwarves any more.

American football is well suited to the American lifestyle – it's perfect for fatally overweight individuals who don't like running. And to be fair, the Scots are doing their best to catch up on Americans' soaring Body Mass Index, and the nation's rate of heart disease would do any Texan proud. But at the end of the day, no matter how much time they spend at TGI Fridays, they are hamstrung by the fact they live in Scotland. Sleet is just not a good replacement for big-name sponsorship.

All of which makes you wonder what draws the supporters of Scottish American football team the Dundee Hurricanes to get into the official supporters' car and spend two hours watching their team swim across the pitch in pursuit of the East Kilbride Pirates. Presumably it's sheer quixotic hope that it might turn out nice and that there will, after all, be dwarves. It's certainly not to visit East Kilbride.

> A SMUG, SUBSTANTIAL, MODERN PLEASURE RESORT – OR RATHER PLEASURE AS THE SCOTS CONCEIVE IT.
>
> Evelyn Waugh on Largs

THE WORLD FAMOUS OLD BLACKSMITH'S SHOP
GRETNA GREEN
DUMFRIES AND GALLOWAY

Once the destination for possibly pregnant lovers in Jane Austen books who sought to be married without their parents' consent, Gretna Green these days is just a small and not especially interesting town just north of the Scottish border.

The town's star attraction is The World Famous Old Blacksmith's Shop, where the lovers of times gone by could, weirdly, seal their matrimony over an anvil; and which is World Famous only in as much as it says so on the sign. Without the sign, it would just be an old blacksmith's shop. At least if Las Vegas stopped offering shotgun marriages, it would still have booze and prostitutes.

Still, the tourist guide for Gretna is scrupulously honest, boasting only that with it having been opened in 1886, 'The World Famous Blacksmith's Shop is one of Scotland's earliest visitor attractions'. This is entirely true, given that 'earliest' doesn't by any stretch of the imagination mean 'best', and 'visitors' can mean anyone from 'tourists' to 'people in search of an urgent marriage due to circumstances beyond their control' to 'mates of the blacksmith'.

The honesty and frankness continues throughout all of Gretna's tourist literature, which seeks to sell the town only as a sort of luxury motorway service station. 'Drive around the shopping centre, passing the picturesque Sculpture Garden surrounded by quaint shopping features, and you arrive at the car park, which is flanked by rolling fields,' reads an excerpt from the front page of the official visitors' guide which can be found discarded in hotel lobbies throughout Gretna.

'The Gateway to Scotland, Gretna Green may be famous for

weddings, but it is also a great place for families and couples to come and enjoy time together experiencing a variety of indoor and outdoor activities including shopping and places to eat. Near to the car park there are two children's play areas, perfect for young people to let off steam after the journey.'

There you have it: a wedding centre, shops, food and a car park, all in one town.

Further equally accurate, equally modest claims include that 'whether you are visiting Gretna Green as part of a wedding or not, it's a great place to break a journey north or south, enjoy as a day visit, or stop for longer and explore the attractions in Carlisle, Hadrian's Wall, the Lake District and Dumfries and Galloway' – in other words, it's a convenient place to stop if you're on your way to a better day out somewhere else.

You thought I was the one? Sorry Gretna, this just isn't going to work. It's not me, it's you.

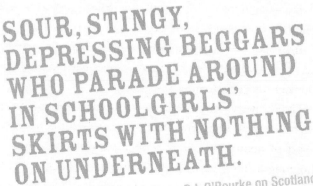

SOUR, STINGY, DEPRESSING BEGGARS WHO PARADE AROUND IN SCHOOLGIRLS' SKIRTS WITH NOTHING ON UNDERNEATH.

P.J. O'Rourke on Scotland

STONEHAVEN OUTDOOR LIDO
NEAR ABERDEEN

If Aberdeen has a reputation, it is not generally for outdoor swimming. Outdoor swimming would be very far down the list of activities that most people would associate with Aberdeen. Punch-ups – they spring to mind. Oil rigs – sure. But taking a dip while the Siberian winds howl around you and a fog descends? No.

Many people campaign to keep our 1930s lidos open; usually these are people who have not been to one. Sure, Aberdeen lido's water is slightly heated, but unless you are planning to spend every second under the surface, be fed through a tube and never come out, that's not a great help.

One of the attractions of the Lido, claim the owners, is that the water is seawater, rather than fresh water, so you had better hope you don't accidentally swallow any. Even though it is filtered, given that it is pumped straight from the North Sea in the vicinity of all those oil rigs – some standing, some not standing so much as they used to – there's a fair chance that it will have contained everything from fish to crude oil. So while a dip in the lido will have given you some exercise, you could go home smelling like a packet of scampi-flavoured Nik-Naks sitting on a petrol station forecourt.

ABERDEEN ... THE EPICENTRE OF GLOOM

Martin Amis

KILMAHOG WOOLLEN MILL
PERTHSHIRE

GENTLEMEN – THE TARTAN

Here's to it!
The fighting sheen of it,
The yellow, the green of it,
The white, the blue of it,
The swing, the hue of it,
The dark, the red of it,
Every thread of it.

The fair have sighed for it,
The brave have died for it,
Foemen sought for it,
Heroes fought for it.
Honour the name of it,
Drink to the fame of it –
THE TARTAN.

Murdoch McClean

Ever wondered how a traditional woollen kilt is made? Or how tweed is woven? Or how Scottish weavers create their distinctive tartan designs?

Really? Oh.

Um, well in that case you'll love the Kilmahog Woollen Mill in Perthshire, a 250-year-old woollen mill complete with its original water mill.

The Kilmahog Mill is a highlight of the Scottish tourist trail, with the toughest Scotsman of modern Britain still proud of the traditional fabric his pretty skirt is made of.

As well as fulfilling every red-blooded male's dream of seeing fabric weaving live, the mill also includes the Clan Tartan Centre, where visitors have the chance to trace their tenuous-at-best Scottish clan history through the medium of patterned fabric.

After you've discovered which clan your cousin's family sort of belongs to and which tartan you should therefore wear, a handy shop will allow you to buy their tartan gifts there and then. That is convenient.

Sure, your teenage daughter might be more used to wearing the latest revealing high street fashions, but she will love wearing that new kilt to parties once you have explained that it is part of her heritage!

So will her brother.

Just in case anyone back at home might doubt your clan heritage, the mill also sells genuine official-looking Clan Certificates suitable both for wall mounting and for use with a freestanding frame. Printed on highest-quality A3 parchment-style paper, these feature a genuine watercolour effect border. Offering an ideal way to silence the sceptics, the certificates are available for just £4.99 from the gift shop.

Doubling as a sort of Scottish heritage shopping mall, the mill also offers a range of other retail opportunities, boasting everything Scotland has to offer that can be sold and put in a carrier bag.

This includes the Spirit of Scotland Whisky Shop, which stocks a range of traditional Scottish malt whiskies, and the Crofters Restaurant, which throughout the day serves a traditional Scottish Breakfast, or as it sometimes colloquially known, 'A Fry-up With Some Haggis Thrown In'.

After a hearty Scottish meal fit for a short-lived long distance lorry driver, it's time to buy some more tartan. Your niece will just love one of those tweed skirts. They're not itchy – they're traditional!

JM BARRIE'S COTTAGE
KIRRIEMUIR
ANGUS

Question: where was JM Barrie born? You know, the bloke who wrote *Peter Pan*. That book about that boy who never gets old. Disney made it into a film. Answer: Kirriemuir!

Yes, household-name Kirriemuir is the birthplace of Peter Pan creator James Matthew Barrie, who immortalised the 'wee red toonie' ('charming little red town', for our readers in Berkshire) as 'Thrums' in his novels *Auld Licht Idylls*, *A Window in Thrums* and *The Little Minister*, according to our sources at Wikipedia.

And while Barrie himself might be long gone – well, we think he is – his memory lives on at the cottage where he was born on the Brechin Road, which is now a museum.

The humble weaver's cottage where Barrie spent the first eight years of his life is said to possibly closely resemble how it would have looked when the Barrie family occupied it, probably, and is complete with a wealth of original artefacts comprising an impressive 33 per cent of a set of six chairs purchased by Barrie's mother on the day of his actual birth in 1860.

As well as offering the visitor the chance to see two of the actual chairs on which Barrie possibly placed both of his buttocks, the museum also boasts other fascinating items including costumes and manuscripts, as well as exhibits such as some shelves probably quite like those on which Barrie kept some of his actual stuff, assuming he had some shelves and kept stuff on them, and an actual clock probably quite like a clock on which he would have read the actual time. He must have had a clock.

Just in case that might appear a little thin, a new exhibition also provides a fascinating insight into the author, and shows how some of his earliest childhood probably – at least possibly – inspired some of his greatest works. Kids can play at being Peter Pan and Tinkerbell in the Peter Pan Playroom while their parents try not to keep looking at their watches and worrying about things such as the price of petrol.

Absorbed by the cottage's collection of family portraits, drawings and its two-chair wealth of original artefacts, it is almost too easy to become part of the 'Never-Never Land' Barrie created and forget about the trials and tribulations of adulthood, such as the long drive back.

As well as seeing Barrie's actual home and some of his actual things (possibly), Kirriemuir also offers the chance to visit Barrie's grave in the local cemetery for some live, up close tombstone action, as well as the chance to see two statues of Peter Pan, his best/only-remembered character.

> **THAT GARRET OF THE EARTH – THAT KNUCKLE END OF ENGLAND – THAT LAND OF CALVIN, OATCAKES AND SULPHUR.**
>
> Sydney Smith on Scotland

NESSIE SPOTTING
LOCH NESS
THE HIGHLANDS

While all of the attractions in this book have been chosen because they are disappointing, most can make one small claim in their favour: they are, at least, real. Unlike Nessie.

Some say the Loch Ness Monster is, as the name suggests, a monster. Others say it is a non-extinct dinosaur which went to sleep for 100 million years. But most people say it is bollocks. This makes Nessie-spotting one of the very worst days out in the last hundred million years of bad days out, involving spending your time waiting for something that will never, ever, ever come.

Like the Abominable Snowman, Sasquatch, the Beast of the Moors and other nonsense, the scientific community regards the Loch Ness Monster as completely made up by bored people in a quiet hilly place. However, it remains one of the most famous examples of 'cryptozoology', the science of investigating made-up animals.

The term 'Loch Ness Monster' was actually coined by Scottish newspaper the *Inverness Courier* in 1933 by Alex Campbell, the water bailiff for Loch Ness.

On 4 August that year, the *Courier* published the claim of a London man, George Spicer, who may have been at the laudanum. He said that a few weeks earlier, while motoring around the Loch, he and his wife had seen 'the nearest approach to a dragon or pre-historic animal that I have ever seen in my life'; presumably nearer than all of the other approaches of dragons or pre-historic animals in Spicer's exciting life. He did have something of a reputation for attracting them. Which didn't go down well in Dundee.

Soon after the story was published, other letters began

225

appearing in the *Courier*, often anonymously, with claims of land or water sightings, either on the writer's part or on the parts of family, friends or other liars. It became something of a must-have publication in the homes of prominent local lunatics.

Eager to fill pages in Britain's primitive newspaper 'silly season', the time when both parliament and the football leagues are on holiday, national journals soon began reporting the stories themselves, which talked of a 'monster fish', 'sea serpent' or 'dragon'.

Anyway, while popular interest in the animal has fluctuated like a giant sea serpent, the Nessie industry has been more or less continuous since.

Nessie-spotting is a regular draw to the towns surrounding the Loch, with Fort Augustus also offering 'a Loch Ness cruise' across the Loch's balmy tropical waters, and the citizens of the village of Drumnadrochit running two separate rival monster museums between them. Now if they could get the two museums to rise up out of the earth and fight each other it would be worth the rail fare.

WALTZING WATERS
NEWTONMORE
THE HIGHLANDS

Owned by an American company that clearly thinks of Britain as a kind of medieval kingdom in which we all wear cloaks and no one has a telly, Waltzing Waters is a 40-minute show of jets of water coming out of pipes – a bit like a bad plumbing job, only upside down.

The water comes out of the pipes at various intervals – some short, some long, others indeterminate. Some of the water is lit up with coloured lights to make it sparkle like the hopeful morning. What makes it all a bit weird, though, is the fact that you are inside. If it was all in the open air, and they were OK-looking fountains, you might sit and watch for five minutes as some music played. But no – this is an actual indoor theatrical event; like *Mamma Mia!* for example. The people of the Highlands, however, apparently prefer the sight of taps set to music.

If you want, you can recreate the Waltzing Waters extravaganza in the comfort of your own bathroom by putting baking soda and red food dye in your shower head. Just turn it on and sit back to enjoy the show. For a special surround-sound version on New Year's Eve, you can put blue dye in your sink taps and toilet flush mechanism and co-ordinate them in time to a Rick Astley CD. If you want to add a sense of excitement and danger, do it while you take a bath holding a toaster plugged into an unsafe electrical socket.

JOHN O'GROATS - BRITAIN'S BIGGEST BASTARDS
JOHN O'GROATS
CAITHNESS

John o'Groats is the site of the most north-easterly bastards in Britain. At the centre of the town is a signpost marked with the direction of Land's End in England's south-west, surrounded by a chain wire. Step inside the chain and you have to pay to take your own photograph.

> "SCOTLAND IS A VILE COUNTRY, THOUGH GOD MADE IT, BUT WE MUST REMEMBER THAT HE MADE IT FOR SCOTSMEN, AND COMPARISONS ARE ODIOUS, BUT GOD ALSO MADE HELL."
>
> Samuel Johnson

SHARMANKA PUPPET THEATRE
GLASGOW

Want to scare the crap out of your kids by teaching them that their toys are possessed by evil spirits that make them come alive in the dark?

THE GREAT THING ABOUT GLASGOW IS THAT IF THERE'S A NUCLEAR ATTACK IT'LL LOOK EXACTLY THE SAME AFTERWARDS.

Billy Connolly

BANNOCKBURN HERITAGE CENTRE AND THE NATIONAL WALLACE MONUMENT
STIRLINGSHIRE

Every true Scottish patriot or slightly aggressive drunk bloke who won't let go of your arm in the street will want you to visit the place where Robert the Bruce defeated Edward II at Bannockburn. If only anyone knew where that was.

Yes, although the great victory for The Bruce in 1314 saw Scotland finally secure the independence which worked out so .well, no one really has much of a clue where it all took place. Still, this isn't considered a problem for the National Trust of Scotland, which is confident enough that it happened 'somewhere or other round here' to have built the Bannockburn Heritage Centre in Stirlingshire.

The Centre features depictions of the coronation of The Bruce as the King of Scotland and of the signing of the Declaration of Arbroath that confirmed Scotland's independence.

Slightly sheepishly, it also features display boards and photographs with the latest information about investigations to find the actual site of the battle.

Still, in for a penny, in for a pound, and as well as an enormous statue of The Bruce there's one of Scotland's other revolutionary hero / part-time sheep-thief William Wallace so that you will keep on getting them mixed up for ever.

Seeing as you have come all this way and you're going to confuse them anyway, you might as well visit The National Wallace Monument nearby, which towers some 67m tall, and looks south to Stirling Castle across Stirling Bridge, the scene of Wallace's greatest victory against the English and one of the best bits in the playing-fast-and-loose-with-history *Braveheart*.

On the first floor of the monument, you can trace Wallace's

story as you try to dissociate what you remember from the film and remind yourself not to talk out loud in a Surrey accent or look a bit English.

After hearing the exciting story of Wallace the rebel leader, you can hear the less exciting story of Adam Smith the economist and political thinker. That's something of a warm-down.

THEY SPEAK OF MY DRINKING, BUT NEVER THINK OF MY THIRST.

Scottish Proverb

THE BRITISH GOLF MUSEUM
ST ANDREWS
FIFE

The university town of St Andrews has a population of more than 16,000, making it only the fifth largest settlement in the already sparsely populated Scottish kingdom of Fife. Of this number, however, roughly a third are students, giving the town one of the highest twat-per-head counts of any town in Britain.

But unless you are a student, or you are visiting a student, or want to drive your car into a bunch of students, St Andrews offers little in the way of entertainment. Its history of crap days out dates back to the 12th century, when the cathedral, the town's main leisure facility, fell into disrepair after the Reformation kicked it in like a sandcastle.

The town's main leisure facility, that is, unless you play golf.

St Andrews has the oldest golf course in the world, The Links, where the game has been excitingly played since the 15th century.

The first written reference to golf in the town is contained in a Charter of 1552, in which one Archbishop Hamilton reserved the right of the St Andrews' townspeople to use the Links land 'for golff, futball, schuteing and all gamis'. He forgot to say 'butt beware: golff does bor the pantes of moste people.'

And with their cathedral ruined by the Reformation, their pubs ruined by students, and their brothels booked up by priests who had nothing to do now that the cathedral was buggered, the townspeople of St Andrews took to the game like no-one else.

The town's status as 'the home of golf' was later enhanced by its Royal and Ancient Golf Club, which was founded in 1754 and which until 2004 exercised legislative authority over the game everywhere in the world except for the US and the mighty golfing nation of Mexico★.

But all this is just the backstory to why St Andrews is also the home of The British Golf Museum – the only thing about golf more dull than watching it.

Are you that person who wondered why a birdie is so called and what it means to play a 'foozle'? Then Dictionary Corner gives the disappointing answer. Or the person interested in golf ball design (spherical is a popular choice)? And so on, room after room, learning all about the game's long, unremarkable history.

After a day of boredom, the memories can be re-lived on the museum's website, which also contains a kids section for children who have been taken against their will to the museum, featuring a gallery of touching, slightly tragic drawings of when daddy stopped knowing they were there.

> **GOLF IS A GOOD WALK SPOILED.**
> Mark Twain

★ whose players decided that they don't need a small town in Scotland to tell them to wear ridiculous trousers and to always lose to the boss.

YURT GLAMPING IN THE CAIRNGORMS

Glamping – short for the oxymoronic 'glamorous camping' – is the new way of acting like an idiot outside a city to amuse people who live nearby. Instead of lying awake at night under nothing but a sheet of 100 per cent porous material stretched paper-thin over a frame while you wonder how many ants have got into your sleeping bag and are now trying to enter your colon, 'glamping' involves spending the nights in well-constructed wooden houses complete with uninterrupted electricity supplies and Smeg kitchens. Just admit the fact that you aren't Ray Mears and don't like camping and check into a hotel. It costs less and is only marginally less comfortable.

For some reason, the basic unit of glamping is the yurt. So not only can you pretend you are camping while you relax with your pizza delivery and WiFi broadband connection, but you can actually pretend that you are Mongolian.

Yes, the Cairngorm Mountains, which have been the scene of countless tragic deaths over the years during climbing expeditions in harsh winter conditions, have now sprouted yurt villages so that social workers from Northampton can pretend they are nomads from the steppes of Central Asia. One company, Canopy and Stars, even advertises yurts filled with Georgian antiques and a roll-top bath – just to really put you in the mindset of the Mongolian Golden Horde sweeping across the plains. Because, as every schoolchild knows, Genghis Khan was responsible for some of the greatest military massacres in history, and after them he liked to relax in his roll-top bath with some of his favourite Georgian knick-knacks around him while listening to Celine Dion doing that song from *Titanic*.

We're not saying there's anything wrong with camping –

there is, loads, but we're not saying that on this specific occasion. But there is a lot wrong with paying to go camping and to stay in a holiday home and to pretend you are a Mongolian peasant farmer who is into early nineteenth-century objets d'art. Perhaps while you're there you can 'till the soil' by using pre-programmed motorised yaks, or you could sub-contract the watching of your herd to a local 'personal herder' while you drink a fine Chablis and talk about share prices.

If you truly want to recreate the Mongolian peasant experience, how about being oppressed by the Soviet Union and dying in your early forties from a preventable disease? We would like to see Canopy and Stars sell that one.

> **CAMPING IS NATURE'S WAY OF PROMOTING THE MOTEL BUSINESS.**
>
> Dave Barry

BAXTERS HIGHLAND VILLAGE
FOCHABERS
MORAY

Like soup? Then you'll love the Visitors Centre at Baxters Foods, where they make soup. As well as the chance to see soup being made, you can stock up on all your Baxters Foods memorabilia at the gift shop before Christmas comes around. Soup is a popular choice.

Baxters Highland Village has something for every member of the family provided that they all have a fairly keen interest in soup.

But the main attraction is the Great Hall where you can experience the magic of the Baxters story through an audio-visual presentation and take the opportunity to sample some of the company's wonderful products, including soup!

WALES

CLIMBING SNOWDON
SNOWDONIA

These days people go for a relaxed, democratic approach to scaling the highest peak in Wales, and it has become traditional to do it in jeans, trainers, T-shirts with witty slogans ('If found, please return to the bar' – priceless!), and carrying a packet of Quavers in case you get hungry. Gone are all the old rules about having at least some of the right equipment and the faintest clue about how to do it, and in their place is self-regard bordering on the criminal and the knowledge that local volunteers will come and carry you down in a sedan chair if you lose your way. (Rather like the tradition of hiring sherpas to do all the hard work running all your stuff up to the top of Everest, where they have a really nice meal ready for you when you arrive, then claiming all the credit for being the first man to scale it. Edmund Hillary, we're talking to you.)

And really, why do you want to get up there anyway? The top of Snowdon is, to put it mildly, bloody cold. The only thing keeping you warm will be the hallucinations of a tropical beach passing before your delusional eyes as the hypothermia sets in and makes the tip of your nose drop off. Seeing camels in front of you playing hopscotch will make you feel really quite unusual.

For some, climbing a mountain is apparently about 'facing your fears' but why anyone should face their fears is open to question. For excellent reasons, we are not best pleased about wrestling a giant squid. Should we face up to our fears and give it a go? No. Unless you are weirdly afraid of a really nice afternoon watching TV while a talented Thai masseuse does wonders for you, your fears, in general, should be left un-faced.

COITY CASTLE
MID GLAMORGAN

A pile of rocks.

> **IT'S IMPOSSIBLE FOR ME TO TELL YOU HOW MUCH I WANT TO GET OUT OF IT ALL. OUT OF THE ETERNAL UGLINESS OF THE WELSH PEOPLE AND ALL THAT BELONGS TO THEM. I'M SICK AND THIS BLOODY COUNTRY'S KILLING ME.**
>
> Dylan Thomas

EISTEDDFOD
WALES

The Eisteddfod, which cannot be pronounced in any language living or dead, is the greatest annual gathering of people who describe themselves as druids. Claiming to be a druid is rather like claiming to be a newt-impersonator or a stamp-hater – people will be pretty sceptical from the very outset that you aren't just making it up.

There is, of course, nothing wrong with celebrating classical Welsh art, such as Tom Jones or Bonnie Tyler. But claiming that singing 'Total Eclipse of the Heart' gives you magical powers is stretching the point.

Ancient Eisteddfods had an interesting function as a poets' test centre, in the more enlightened days when bards and poets actually had to be licensed by the state. They would perform a few ditties and if they remained unpunched by the third verse, they were allowed to move on to writing letters to the *Daily Telegraph* about which leaves they had seen in their gardens that day.

Druidry has seen a renaissance in recent years as people with a lot of time on their hands have been attracted to the promise of ancient magic and mystery while 300 men dressed in white robes and hats chant in a sinister unknown language. Just don't invite any of your black friends who grew up in Mississippi in the 1950s. They might not see the funny side.

ABERYSTWYTH CAMERA OBSCURA
WALES

The Victorians were into some pretty strange things, such as putting stockings on table legs so that the hussyish furniture wouldn't excite gentlemen any more than was proper. Bathing machines – they were a bit nutty too.

Our great-great grandfathers also had an odd liking for falsely claiming things were further away than they actually were. This is where the Aberystwyth Camera Obscura came in. These oddities were small rooms on hills where a system of mirrors would project an image of a nearby scene onto a table in the room. So instead of having to go to all the trouble of pretending they were miles away from the town and it looked really small from where they were standing, they could instead nip up one of the town's hills to use what amounts to a big periscope which projects a quite small image of the town onto a table. Just as if it were miles away. They could then stroke their beards and discuss how many days' journey the town must be from where they were.

Of course, most people who have been to Aberystwyth claim it looks better from a distance – ideally a substantial distance. But that doesn't quite explain why you wouldn't just leave and look at it in the rear-view mirror.

FOR WALES, SEE ENGLAND.

Encyclopaedia Britannica, 1888

BOG SNORKELLING
LLANWRTYD WELLS
WALES

For most people, drowning in mud is an unpleasant idea. But for the locals of the village of Llanwrtyd Wells it's a great way to spend a Sunday afternoon. And not only is Llanwrtyd Wells the home of immersing yourself in wastewater, it also hosts the annual world championships. That's right, there are people out there who actually compete at social exclusion.

Of course it all seems a bit of a laugh until you submerge yourself in freezing, stinking Welsh bog water. Under the rules of bog snorkelling you are not allowed to use a recognised swimming stroke; but it is conventional to panic, kick wildly with your feet and scream into your snorkel at the thought that you are shortly to die, miles from civilisation at the bottom of a Welsh bog. Many participants like to bargain with God that if He lets them get out of this alive, He can take their mother instead. She's old and it's her turn. And if she dies, you'll get the house, so it's swings and roundabouts really.

Interestingly, Llanwrtyd Wells is also the host of the equally absurd annual Man Vs Horse cross-country race. Over a course of 22 miles, men race against horses. Yes, real ones. If you fancy a wager on it, here's a hot tip: bet on the horses.

LLECHWEDD SLATE CAVERNS
SNOWDONIA

The fascinating story of slate.

> "A WRETCHED PEOPLE [THE WELSH], THEY KNOW LITTLE, HAVE SEEN LESS, AND THEY CANNOT BE TAUGHT."
>
> Sir Philip Sidney, *An Apology For Poetry*, 1595

TOP TEN-
'IT LOOKED MUCH NICER ON TV

1) Goathland, Yorkshire – *Heartbeat*
The only accurate point in the series is that the locals are anything but friendly and there is crime. It also has a silly name.

2) Oxford – *Inspector Morse*
There's a lot more traffic, and millions more Old Etonians guffawing.

3) Peckham, London – *Only Fools and Horses*
Far from being full of loveable cockney rascals as in its TV depiction (see satellite channel UK TV Gold any time, every day for details), real-life Peckham is so dangerous the BBC had to film the series in Bristol.

4) Glasgow – *Taggart*
The series portrays the town as a heroin-filled corpse-littered slag heap. Which is seeing it through rose-tinted spectacles.

5) Bath – *Pride and Prejudice*
Bath hasn't seen the sun since 1922.

6) Notting Hill, London – *Notting Hill*
A small independent bookshop would never survive in Notting Hill. The rent would bankrupt anyone not selling lattes at £50 a pop.

7) Jersey – *Bergerac*

The local police spend their entire careers hoping for a murder. You are far more likely to die from boredom.

8) Liverpool – *Boys from the Black Stuff*

The reality is far more depressing and Liverpudlians never shut up about the Beatles who left as soon as they could afford to.

9) Chester – *Hollyoaks*

The cast of Hollyoaks have hard bodies and chiselled features. The people of Chester have giros and bad teeth.

10) Holmfirth, Yorkshire – *Last of the Summer Wine*

You can pay a quite staggering amount of money to stay in the Nora Batty Experience, the terraced house that the character lived in. Despite the fact that she isn't real, and therefore didn't live anywhere.

RHONDDA HERITAGE PARK BLACK GOLD TOUR
RHONDDA VALLEY

The Rhondda Heritage Park in Wales is a former colliery, which offers a simulated trip down a mine. Quite why you would want to simulate such a trip when you can do the actual thing at a working colliery and get paid for it (known in industrial circles as 'working as a miner') is not explained by their marketing material.

If the park were to provide a genuine simulated coal-mining experience, it should probably go the whole hog and expose you to dangerous underground gases, occasional shaft collapses killing your young friends in front of your eyes, and an unexpected closure of the park followed by a bus ride to a nearby job centre staffed by uncaring 19-year-olds.

After that you and your surviving mates could spit on a photograph of Margaret Thatcher ripped from a magazine before in-fighting drives you to establish rival trade unions which set you at each other's throats. From there, you can relax at the local infirmary. So long as it hasn't also closed.

As part of a weekend itinerary aimed at school parties for their GCSE in Dangerous Employment Studies, this could be combined with sending unhappy orphans up chimneys, and lethal 14-hours shifts dodging heavy machinery in an Indonesian sweat shop.

THE SMALLEST HOUSE IN BRITAIN
CONWY

Promises little; delivers it.

> MRS POWELL'S FIRST COUSIN HAD LEFT PATAGONIA AND GONE BACK HOME TO WALES. 'HE HAS DONE WELL,' SHE SAID. 'HE'S NOW THE ARCHDRUID!'
>
> Bruce Chatwin, *In Patagonia*

CENTRE FOR ALTERNATIVE TECHNOLOGY
POWYS

The real problem with the Centre for Alternative Technology (CAT) is that it is not nearly alternative enough. It's not like it's alien technology that allows you to splice your DNA with a monkey and grow a tail for a day, which would be excellent.

Also quite good would be to head in the other direction in a 'steam punk' theme like *The League of Extraordinary Gentlemen* and design submarines that look like Georgian townhouses and are powered by top-hatted gentlemen on Penny Farthings. However, it's really just about keeping the amount of energy we use each day to a minimum. There are housing estates in Middlesbrough where they are decades ahead of the CAT on that score. The CAT can't compete with 'A quick trip down the Job Centre Plus to sign on and back to Jeremy Kyle, I think.'

The centre was founded in 1973 and, oddly, one of its first visitors was the Duke of Edinburgh. Presumably he had temporarily run out of endangered animals to shoot and had heard there were some hippies running around in Wales without natural cover.

In 2010 the CAT was very proud to be awarded the *Daily Telegraph* award for Best Building, won for a round brown building that looks quite a lot like a gas storage tower on the side of a multi-storey car park, if you ask us.

There is now a small community of people who actually live at CAT, presumably in 'alternative' ways, such as wearing hats on their knees and pretending that Portugal doesn't exist. Well, it's certainly an alternative to being at all sensible.

The community apparently 'lives as a co-operative' (and there we were thinking it would be run as a capitalist dictatorship based on family wealth, power and ruthless greed). You have to wonder why more freeloaders don't take advantage of such set-ups. You should be able to get at least three days out of it before they rumble you. That must be long enough for a bath and a hot meal, even if it is a vegan one. Entertainment might be restricted to 'traditional ethnic storytelling' by people brought up in Luton, though.

If you get tired of the whole thing – perhaps you miss your leather jacket and not wincing every time you eat something – and want to go out in style, you could always let it slip that you had spent the previous day with the Young Conservatives, followed by an afternoon at Stringfellows; and plan to spend the forthcoming evening watching your DVD box-set of *Love Thy Neighbour* before reading Enoch Powell's autobiography. They might actually melt.

> THE SORT OF PLACE THAT INSPIRED OLD-FASHIONED FEARS OF SEASIDE CRIME. IT MADE ME THINK OF POISONING AND SUFFOCATION, SCREAMS BEHIND CLOSED DOORS, PETS SCRATCHING AT THE WAINSCOTTING.
>
> Paul Theroux on Llandudno, Wales

IRELAND

BELFAST PRIDE
NORTHERN IRELAND

The battle for mainstream acceptance of homosexuality has been long fought and hard won. We take our hats off to those involved. And that's why at Belfast's annual Pride march, liberal folk look on in horror as all their work teaching their kids that gay people are just like everyone else is undone by 200 men in tiny leather jockstraps.

Members of 'specialist' political or religious groups rub their hands and sharpen their pitchforks when Pride rolls around again. Not only is it another 16-page colour pull-out feature in their parish magazine sorted, but if Pride doesn't scare the bejeesus out of parishioners, sending them running to the safety of the nearest chapel, furiously crossing themselves, nothing will.

The main way Pride brings people together is in the unlikely 48-hour alliance between Ian Paisley and the Pope, briefly uniting them in fury before they ease back into their preferred state of mutual hatred.

> AMONG THE COUNTLESS BLESSINGS I THANK GOD FOR, MY FAILURE TO FIND A HOUSE IN IRELAND COMES FIRST.
>
> Evelyn Waugh

KISSING THE BLARNEY STONE
BLARNEY CASTLE
CORK

Slightly less hygienic than drinking from a sewer or visiting a Thai bordello with a devil-may-care attitude, kissing the Blarney Stone is an experience not to be missed if contracting preventable diseases is your thing.

It remains one of few tourist experiences where you should take penicillin before, during, and after the experience. You should also be checked by a GP within 48 hours.

Planting your lips on this unremarkable piece of rock doesn't just put you in danger of unpleasant DNA transfer, however, because in order to gain access to it, you must lean backwards over a 70m precipice in Blarney Castle, with all the vertiginous fun that can entail. You have a helper to hold on to you while you do this though. You just have to hope that 'Old Bob' is a teetotaller.

Kissing the stone is supposed to make you believable when talking rubbish. It is therefore possibly the only leisure attraction in the world to admit that its own marketing is based on fantasy.

Blarney Castle has other offerings, though, such as what it describes as 'the magical and mystical Rock Close'. Now just remind me: what was it the Blarney Stone does again? Oh yes, it enables you to talk bollocks. The Rock Close of Liars is strikingly similar to an unremarkable small piece of the countryside. Constituting a hole in a big rock, through which one can walk, just doesn't scream 'magical and mystical'; it screams 'geological'. But that didn't stop one Croften Croker writing in his 1824 thriller *Researches in the South of Ireland*: 'I know of no place where I could sooner imagine these little elves holding their moon-light revelry.' Readers may submit their own nominations for where little elves hold their moon-light revelry – care of the publisher.

ST PATRICK'S DAY
DUBLIN

As every Irishman knows, St Patrick was a devout bully of reptiles, and for this deed he is honoured with an annual festival of drinking.

The yearly ritual sees tens of thousands of Irish folk from America descend on Dublin to ask why the locals are not all speaking Gaelic and doing the Riverdance as they expected. While they are there shops sell out of green food dye to pour into Guinness, just like they saw Mel Gibson do when he freed Ireland from Germany in *Braveheart*.

Yes, for three months in advance, 'Irishmen' from all over the world go to Wikipedia to see where Ireland is and what the capital is called, before coming 'home' to reconnect with the land of their great aunt's birth. To feel the soil beneath their feet. And the pavement – then the hospital sheets – beneath their backs.

St Patrick's Day has been celebrated in Dublin ever since it was founded and hardly a year goes by without Dublin city council remembering that it is coming up and they should probably do something about it because the tourists seem to like it.

The day and the festival that now surround it are about bringing people together in celebration of someone they know nothing about except that he has a day. So during this period lasting precisely 24 solar hours, all visitors – young, old, standing up, sitting down – raise a toast to the motherland before looking up the times of their flights home. And on this day any man who spills another man's drink is asking for a fight, and by Jesus he's going to get one. But the Irish are very accommodating people and they will always find somewhere for you to sleep: the police cells, the supermarket trolley collection area, the space between two parked cars – every available piece of concrete ground is pressed into service that night to provide makeshift beds for the revellers.

Wow! What a day!

FACTFILE: ST GEORGE'S DAY
Irishmen, Americans and Guinness Company shareholders might love to celebrate St Patrick's Day, but across the water in England there is growing support for an event to mark St George's Day. England's patron saint, George, was actually half Roman, half Israeli; and while the tale of Patrick kicking out all the snakes from Ireland might seem a bit unlikely, George is said to have made his name killing a dragon. The big fibber.

> **IRELAND. THE BIG ISSUE SELLER OF EUROPE.** A.A. Gill

ULSTER AMERICAN FOLK PARK
OMAGH, CO. TYRONE

You don't need to visit the Ulster American Folk Park to understand quite what's wrong with it. You see, the clue is in the name. It's an attraction dedicated to American folk traditions ... in Ulster. Ulster may have been fought over for generations, but never by America, which has never laid claim to it.

But don't visit the park in search of an answer to the question of quite why the people of Ulster should be more interested in American folk traditions than they are in, say, the folk traditions of Italy, or in archery, or in the recorded work of French synthesiser musician Jean-Michel Jarre.

Instead of answering it, the park merely bats the question away with a reference to the fact that many people emigrated to the United States from Ireland, before whisking you on to the exhibits before you ask any more awkward questions such as whether there are any more public tourist attractions nearby.

The list of events held at the park includes Thanksgiving Day, 'when Americans all over the world turn their thoughts to home and family as they prepare to celebrate Thanksgiving'. True, but the point is that they are Americans, not Irishmen.

Confused? Well shut up and enjoy the 'Days of Christmas Past' event, which 'takes the family back in time to experience the magic of a traditional Christmas' – which is all good fun, but has nothing much to do with American folk traditions in or out of Ulster.

At the time of writing you can visit 'Christmas in Castletown', which uses archive photographs and film footage 'to explore the emigrant experience of Christmas as told in the songs of Bing Crosby to Shane MacGowan'. Bing Crosby is included because his maternal great-grandparents were Irish.

We're not joking. And we're not entirely convinced that Shane MacGowan – who is from Kent and went, briefly, to Westminster, one of England's poshest public schools – ever emigrated from Ulster to America.

As you tour the exhibits, which are spread over 40 acres of rambling parkland, the whole experience seems more and more like a long anecdote from an elderly relative who has drunk his bodyweight in sherry.

'Interested in American Folk traditions? Then you'll love the "Through The Eye of a Needle" exhibition, which celebrates the history of the sewing needle and all its creations. Mostly textiles. Hang on, what was I saying? Oh yes, it includes embroidered pictures and needlework samplers from the eighteenth and nineteenth centuries and some …'

Having allowed itself the themes of Ireland, America, emigration, migration generally, rural and town life, and the eighteenth, nineteenth and twentieth centuries, there isn't really much that the park can't cover. But what it never explains is why it chose to.

> **I RECKON NO MAN IS THOROUGHLY MISERABLE UNLESS HE BE CONDEMN'D TO LIVE IN IRELAND.**
>
> Jonathan Swift

NATIONAL AND INTERNATIONAL

MAYDAY BANK HOLIDAY
YOUR NEAREST MOTORWAY
SERVICE STATION

There's little doubt that this is not what you were planning, but the motorway service station is definitely where you are going to end up after three hours sitting in near-stationary traffic on the M1. Luckily, from the all-day breakfast priced to make the Sultan of Brunei gasp in amazement to the desolate AA man at the door offering 'to yourself' the basic package for a reduced rate, they are all the bloody same. So once you have been to one you can drop into any other and feel like you are home – so long as you charge yourself £8.95 for breakfast each morning and you've run out of toast.

Contrary to what Heston Blumenthal would have you believe, this goes just as much for the Little Chef at Popham in Hampshire. Heston, you see, transformed this littlest of chefs for an odd TV programme in 2009 and it has somehow made its way into the *Good Food Guide*. At first, this sounds like a heartwarming underdog tale of a plucky little café taking on the gastronomic big boys. Rubbish. It's a stomach-turning tale of the *Good Food Guide* trying to get a bit of free publicity by sticking a crappy motorway service station into the book in the hope that the *Telegraph* will run the story on a slow news day.

They were right. Sometimes life is just predictably awful.

THE UK ROCK PAPER SCISSORS CHAMPIONSHIP
VARIOUS VENUES

'You'll never guess what I got up to last night!'

'Um, I don't mean to be rude, it's just that I have to finish these reports today, and – '

'Go on, guess!'

'You just told me that I won't be able to do so.'

'Guess!'

'Did you go to the UK Rock Paper Scissors Championship?'

'Um … yeah. How did you know that?'

A magnet for you–don't-have-to-be-mad-to-work-here-but-it-helps types across Britain, the UK Rock Paper Scissors Championship is where wacky went to die.

Now an annual event, the 2010 Championship was held at the Durrell Arms pub in Fulham, west London, marking the world's single biggest labouring of a moderately amusing joke since the 2009 competition.

For those unfamiliar with the term, Rock Paper Scissors is a simple, instant means of settling a decision in the vein of tossing a coin if that coin had three sides and each side beat one of the other sides, but lost to the side it didn't beat.

According to spurious fact boxes of the kind that you might see accompanying an article about the event in a local newspaper, the game dates back to the Chinese Han Dynasty in around 200 BC, and in other languages is known variously as 'fargling', 'cachi-pun', 'burung-batu-air' and 'jan-ken-pon'.

Always, scissors cuts paper to win, but then paper wraps stone, and stone blunts scissors. Simple. Fair. Not fun to watch.

Really milking Rock Paper Scissors' entertainment value, however, the UK Championship sees competitors go head-to-head from 5pm until shortly before pub closing time in a series of best-of-three contests between blokes who work in IT and enjoy these nights out. For people who want to suck every atom of fun out of a game which already has it in short supply, you can even play it on your computer against your computer.

The utterly bonkers UK Championship is just one of a number of equally stark-raving-mad Rock Paper Scissors events held across the world but mostly in America. But while it isn't original, at least it's mercifully short, unlike the US National Xtreme RPS Competition, which dragged the joke out across a series of contests in 2007 and 2008.

With most countries having got bored by the decade's end, no World Championships were held in 2010, making the UK Championship the most prestigious/only event in the Rock, Paper Scissors calendar that year.

UK champion Paul Lewis has moved from working in database-driven to web-based integration systems and is currently growing a moustache.

POST-SCRIPT: THE MASPRO DENKOH CORPORATION OF JAPAN

Rock Paper Scissors doesn't HAVE to be unfunny. In 2005, when Takashi Hashiyama, president of the Maspro Denkoh Corporation in Japan, struggled to choose between Christie's and Sotheby's to sell the company's collection of impressionist paintings including works by Cézanne, Picasso and Van Gogh, he made them play the game.

Christie's chose scissors after researching the psychology of the game and consulting the children of a number of its arts specialists, beating Sotheby's, which offered paper after concluding that playing the game was humiliating enough for international experts on impressionism without having to 'research' it and ask children for advice.

THE CARAVAN CLUB

Desperate and ashamed teenagers horrified by the thought of public reaction to the news that their families are dragging them away on a Caravan Club weekend, sometimes try to convince their friends that these rallies really are sex-fuelled orgies of abandon. The reality is more like a damp and freezing orgy of mutual loathing in a confined space, broken only by the frequent need to have your toilet pumped out into a big underground vat.

The Caravan Club has a million members, a staff of more than 800 and an annual turnover of £100m. The mind boggles, really.

Kids love the open air. So keeping them in a single unstable room ventilated only by holes in the fabric of the vehicle for 48 hours will drive them nuts. At the very least they will hate their parents even more than they were planning to anyway. If caravan parks really want to make money, they should have on-site divorce lawyers.

CHRISTMAS PANTOS WITH CHRISTOPHER BIGGINS

No one is really sure how he does it, but all Christmas pantos star Christopher Biggins. An Ugly Sister, an Ugly Mother, an Ugly Passer-By, you name it and it's in Biggins's chameleon-like repertoire. He is rumoured to have had a network of high-speed monorail tunnels constructed between all British seaside towns so he can appear on cue in seven different shows simultaneously each night. He did this with the money he got from acting in *Porridge*, which he invested wisely.

Provincial theatres need Biggins like a fish needs water. They literally breathe Biggins. Without him they would curl up and die, flapping about like mackerel. Local theatres, after all, rely on a clientele older than the pyramids to keep going, and Biggins packs the coffin-dodgers in like there's no tomorrow. For many, of course, there won't be.

The panto has a loyal clientele with an annual mortality rate of around 60 per cent so, yes, there is a drive to sell tickets earlier and earlier each year. They usually go on sale about three years in advance, on pension day, before it's all madly blown on clocks with cats on and 12 pairs of comfortable fur-lined boots advertised by Christopher Sodding Biggins in *The People's Friend*.

Each time one of the audience croaks during a show, the first person to notice is usually the bored teenage usherette who has to inform the management that another one has gone and Snow White isn't on yet so could some of the dwarves help with dragging out the corpse. They're only little so they can carry her on their shoulders and no one will notice. This move is known in theatrical circles as 'midget mayhem'.

Everyone knows when it's his time to go. Except for Biggins. He never bloody leaves.

SWIMMING THE CHANNEL

Now that humans have pretty much mastered the art of getting from Dover to France without freezing to death – we even have wonderful machines that fly through the sky like birds – you have to wonder why some people insist on doing it covered in bear fat and limping along behind a dedicated motor boat that could so easily just take them over with a lot less bother and hoo-ha.

No one is more surprised by this sight than the tens of thousands of Afghans and Iraqis camped out on the shores of Calais, desperately hoping that a lorry with a none-too-observant driver will trundle past on its way to the ferry. They just aren't expecting a middle-class actor with a large house in Hampstead to do it in the other direction without a boat.

Given the amount of effort they are about to put into getting across the Channel, it actually seems a bit rude to endanger your own life to do the precise opposite. It's like you're rubbing their noses in your legal right to cross the Channel even in the most ludicrous fashion imaginable. If you could do it dressed as a gorilla wearing a nappy you probably would, so long as they would see it.

In fact, next time you fancy spending 10 hours in the freezing, murky brown water doing exactly what you could do in 45 minutes on a car ferry, why not tease them a bit by not quite touching the land, then swimming back a bit, coming in once again, reaching out your hand to grasp the soil, then pulling it back etc. Then when you get onto land, you could show your passport around and then laugh as you saunter off to a nice restaurant which you can easily afford.

THE SEALED KNOT BATTLE RE-ENACTMENTS

The Sealed Knot, which re-enacts battles from the English Civil War and other historical conflicts, is a useful organisation for the police. They know exactly who they have to keep tabs on in case there is a spate of brutal murders using a mace. Instead of all that dull knocking on doors and television appeals stuff, they can just have a quick scan through the Sealed Knot's membership list to see who lives locally and hasn't been banged up for the last 14 months. These are, after all, people who have been obsessed with battleaxes far more than the average member of society ever since the Territorial Army rejected their applications. And yet, the one place they don't seem to indulge their interest in beheadings is on the battlefield, where it could be deemed at least partially acceptable – certainly more so than the car park behind Netto where they usually do it.

Of course, were The Sealed Knot day-release crazies to truly re-enact the Battle of Naseby, they would need to massacre 1,000 men in fancy hats, and even the most rabid haters of fancy hats would baulk at a slaughter on that scale. It would, however, make for one hell of a spectacle. The dead and dying having their fingers hacked off for rings while their harridan wives happily shag the victors and their kids sell their shoes to passers-by would also add to the historical accuracy of the scene, but you aren't likely to see it. Unless you go for their special late-night 'anything-goes' performances.

KILLING KITTENS – THE POSH SWINGERS CLUB

In the good old days, when one fancied a bit of rumpy pumpy with a lady who was not one's wife, one would organise a little bit of suburban wife swapping. Just a bit of fun. No pressure. It starts at eight if you're free. Bring a bottle.

Such events usually took place in Surrey in the 1970s, when clothes were flammable. It may have made you weep a little inside that it had come to this – Beryl, from Number 48, who had already had four kids and a serious nervous breakdown – but at least it was free. No longer. Now, if you are part of the Beautiful Set and once met Kate Middleton's sister, you must – *must* – attend a Killing Kittens shagathon. These take place either in a Mayfair townhouse or a Scottish castle whose owner thought he was letting it to a historical society and gets back to find the most unpleasant things in his newspaper rack. Things that he recognises but doesn't want to touch.

According to bad newspaper articles, these days, if you haven't paid £400 to do it with a strange – often very strange – stockbroker from Chelsea in front of a crowd of people, you literally haven't lived.

Killing Kittens bills itself as 'the club for the world's sexual elite'. That means it is for people who laugh at the lack of challenge in a basic sexual situation, instead heading directly for the super-advanced options, such as landing a plane blindfolded while having a three-up with a pair of twins. It does not bill itself as 'a money-raking big ball of hype that really consists of 45 podgy public schoolboys who paid £150 each to come here in the hope that they might find some girl drunk enough to hump them, and go home again frustrated and feeling rejected just like every other time this has happened'. But it should.

The owners certainly know their market: people on the

wrong side of 'plain' and the right side of 'loaded'. Participants have to wear a mask to the parties. Why? Not for the romance but, you suspect, for more practical reasons regarding basic human instinct. One wonders, also, what would happen if you turned up in a *Scream* mask. Perhaps in a full-length black cloak and carrying what appears to be a blood-soaked knife. But you had paid your £150 entry and you want to come in, thank you very much. 'What? The knife? Oh no!' you laugh gaily. 'That's just for protection. Besides, she was asking for it.'

> " CONTINENTAL PEOPLE HAVE SEX LIFE; THE ENGLISH HAVE HOT-WATER BOTTLES.
>
> George Mikes, *How to be an Alien* "

NAKED BIKE RIDES / PROTESTS / MASS PHOTOGRAPHS
SEEMINGLY EVERYWHERE

Due to what must be the cruellest stroke of nature, Britain is one of the few countries unlucky enough to actually become colder due to global warming, as the Gulf Stream stops and thinks for a bit before saying: 'Actually, you know what? This year I fancy hitching up my pleasantly warming skirt, completely by-passing Britain altogether and just adding to the beach fun for the Spanish. After all, they're the ones who really need me.'

And yet, as the mercury plummets right through the bottom of the thermometer, onto the floor below, scaring the hell out of the cat, it seems people are getting more naked by the minute.

In a single month around the end of the year you can go naked rambling in Lancashire, join a naked bike ride in Hull, go on a naked protest in London or join 1,000 other unclothed oddballs to have your photo taken at a national landmark by an American photographer/probable pervert/fugitive from justice. Every one is an opportunity to compare yourself to much more attractive people and come away with a little less confidence than you started with, but a few more 'useful' mental images than you had this morning.

Naked bike rides also provide you with saddle burn; and God help you if you become separated from the group and have an accident, because you will have a lot of explaining to do before the ambulance crew come anywhere near you.

FACTFILE: NAKED PROTESTS
In April 2010 two dozen women held a topless protest in the US city of Portland. For hours they paraded around the town

demanding 'equal-opportunity public toplessness'. They weren't calling for the right to be naked from the waist up – they already had that because men had insisted on it years before – the spectacle was to demand that blokes stop staring at them when they did so.

The event's organiser, Ty MacDowell, said it was to draw attention to the fact that a topless woman shouldn't attract any more attention than a topless man. Interestingly, the march attracted a crowd of more than 500 men who lined the streets to cheer in encouragement. Afterwards, MacDowell said she had been 'amazed and enraged' by the fact that large numbers of heterosexual males would come along to see 24 attractive young women walking about topless. She was especially astonished that they had been taking photos and video footage.

In order to show them how wrong they were to do so, she announced that she would hold a second similar protest. When she made the announcement the assembled males were so ashamed of their previous actions that they gave a massive cheer at the chance to make amends at a second rally, and assured her they would be there, no matter what the circumstances, but they hoped it would be cold weather and suggested the girls huddle together for warmth.

ULTIMATE FRISBEE

Obviously replaces 'Penultimate Frisbee', which was deemed outdated. Ultimate Frisbee is to sport what humming is to music.

> **THE ENGLISH ARE NOT HAPPY UNLESS THEY ARE MISERABLE, THE IRISH ARE NOT AT PEACE UNLESS THEY ARE AT WAR, AND THE SCOTS ARE NOT AT HOME UNLESS THEY ARE ABROAD.**
>
> George Orwell

SPONSORED PARACHUTE JUMPS

Perhaps this entry doesn't belong in this book – after all, a sponsored parachute jump is a fantastic day out. The thrill, the rush. The thing is, it's a pretty crap day for the poor sods who are paying for the experience.

If Paul wants to do a parachute jump, just why should you be paying for it? You can see what's in it for Paul, but what exactly is in it for you?

Sure, Cancer Research is a good cause – as is Aids research, Malaria research or, for that matter, pretty much any kind of research that doesn't involve Iran and missile payloads. But if Paul wants to do a parachute jump, he can pay for it. If he can't pay for it, perhaps he could get a job, and then pay for it. It seems unfair that you are the one getting the job to pay for it. You wonder who paid for Paul's last holiday and suspect it was his parents.

In fact, it's almost as if Paul doesn't really care about the 'giving money to charity' part and just wants a free parachute jump. It's almost as if Paul is secretly a bit of a freeloading bastard. If he were playing a sponsored game of Russian roulette, you might just consider it.

The same goes for other selfish charitable causes: sponsored treks through the Himalayas by people who really want to trek through the Himalayas but don't want to pay for it; sponsored climbs of huge rock formations on beautiful Greek islands by keen rock climbers who fancy a free holiday; sponsored tea parties attended by people who like scones and don't want to stump up the cash. The list goes on.

You can test this theory: when Paul asks you to sign underneath all the fake names on his form, just say you would be happy to help but that instead of giving him the cash, you will give it straight to the charity. That way he won't have to spend so much time collecting the money from all his sponsors, which must be a bit of a bore, and the charity will save on administration costs.

You can also print off a series of adverts that you found on the internet for jobs for which he is well qualified, and point out how much money he could raise for his chosen charity if instead of spending four weeks on holiday in – sorry, trekking through – Peru, he stayed here and worked for a month. Ask him why he isn't doing it that way round. See what his face does.

An alternative method for dealing with Paul is to have your own sponsorship sheet ready. Knowing that he is making the rounds of your office, you should prepare one with a few names on it – preferably entirely false ones you can claim to be distant relatives of yours – promising you very large amounts of money in return for completing a task far more arduous than his own. For instance Margaret Fellows (a good name to pick because it sounds solid and believable) has sponsored you £85 for your sponsored four-week trek through the Gobi Desert. None of the other names on the list have gone below £70 in their promised sums. When Paul comes calling, you can whip out your own form and suggest that if you sponsor him, he sponsors you.

FLASH MOBS

Perhaps there was once something very slightly interesting about sudden gatherings of people in places that The Man wasn't expecting. But as soon as the advertising bozos cottoned on to a new way to push their wares to the congenitally persuadable by getting 2,000 strangers to moonwalk in Liverpool Street station for a T-Mobile advert, the lifeblood was sucked out of it faster than a leech on a really good day.

In fact soon life imitated art imitating life when 12,000 people with a substantial amount of time on their hands turned up at Liverpool Street to recreate the advert. A City of London Police spokeswoman said: 'It was a peaceful and fun event.'

You know you're onto a serious winner when the police describe your counter-cultural happening as 'peaceful and fun'.

" THE ENGLISH THINK SOAP IS CIVILISATION.

Heinrich von Treitschke, German philosopher

"

MORRIS DANCING
AT A VILLAGE FÊTE NEAR YOU

Ah, Morris Dancing … God's gift to comedians.

For those unfamiliar with the bizarre practice, Morris Dancing is a tradition in which men don straw hats and poorly woven shirts, attach bells to their ankles and dance in circles shouting 'Hey nonny nonny!' until they are knocked to the ground by passers-by. At least they are in the more enlightened North of England.

Originating in the fourteenth century and all but happily extinguished by the turn of the twentieth century, Morris Dancing came back into popular consciousness in the 1970s, when Britain's folk revival saw a new interest in awful British traditions. The Morris is seen by Morris Men as a proud tradition that has been resurrected from history – although if hanging were to be resurrected from history, of course, hangmen would feel the same way.

Seeing Morris Men perform is a crap day out for the English only because, in fairness to them, no Scotsman, Irishman or Welshman would go in for that sort of shit. Men who dance the Morris are typically white English history teachers who vote Lib Dem. Tied in with their nostalgia for English folk traditions is a passion for real ale or traditional cider. They are the sort of men who address the person behind the bar as 'My good barkeep' or 'Fair lass' without expecting to piss off everyone in the pub and have their pies deliberately sneezed on in the kitchen.

Their drinks of choice – obscure liquids only mentioned in restricted-print-run circulars from the Campaign for Real Ale – usually taste milder than the chemical-filled lager popular with the mainstream 17-year-old male but are often far, far stronger; which is fortunate if your day plan comprises jigging to a penny whistle. If you don't already get it, you never will.

For the children of Morris Men, and in particular teenage children of Morris Men who try to keep their friends from finding out by saying their parents are divorced and they never see their dads, being told that dancing the Morris is an old English tradition typically only confirms their suspicion that the past was rubbish. Paying £15 to get into a nightclub that smells of armpits to dance to recorded music created on a pinball machine isn't great, but at least you don't have to strap bells to your ankles, and there's a sporting chance you might meet a member of another sex jaded enough to give you a go.

Morris Men will counter, however, that for all its apparent tweeness, like the May Pole, the Morris is symbolic of ancient pagan fertility rites, and is highly charged with subtle sexual undertones. Yet true as this may be, nothing ancient is fertile, and no man wearing pyjamas with bells on the ankles is getting laid any time soon. Sorry.

For family members, discovering that their father or husband is a Morris Man can be a devastating experience, leading many Morris Men to hide their secret longing from their families, meeting up in secluded fields to answer their secret passion. In this way, dancing the Morris is much like the practice of sexual voyeurism known as 'dogging', only less sordid, and more embarrassing. In some parts of Cumbria local groups of Dogging Men have therefore sprung up as front organisations.